I Married A JUNKIE

Put to The Ultimate Test by Addiction, Love, and Life

DR. CALI ESTES & TIM ESTES

CHECKMATE PRESS
checkmatepress.com

Checkmate Press books are published by:

McLean Media Group, LLC
4364 Glenwood Dr.
Bozeman, MT 59718

I Married A Junkie/ Dr. Cali Estes & Tim Estes. -- 1st ed.
ISBN 978-1-7321781-0-6

The Publisher has strived to be as accurate and complete as possible in the creation of this book.

This book is not intended for use as a source of legal, business, health, or medical advice. All readers are advised to seek services of competent professionals in legal, business, and health or medical fields.

While all attempts have been made to verify information provided in this publication, the Publisher assumes no responsibility for errors, omissions, or contrary interpretation of the subject matter herein. Any perceived slights of specific persons, peoples, or organizations are unintentional.

This book is dedicated to Willie S.,
aka Leggz, for saving Tim's life.

Thank you also to Tina Ortiz and Bob Sellers
of Ortiz-Sellers Photography for their
generous gift of professional wedding
photography services and her karmic duties.

(She thought Tim looked like Brett Michaels
and her daughter *loves* Brett Michaels.)

CONTENTS

FOREWORD by Matt Bradley ix

PROLOGUE 1

PART I: Growing Up in the American Dream 5

PART II: Living the Dream 41

PART III: Living the Nightmare 83

PART IV: Stuck in a Lucid Nightmare 117

PART V: The Awakening 155

EPILOGUE 173

FOREWARD

I was impressed with this book from the very start. To step into Dr. Cali Estes' and her husband Tim's lives is to take an incredible journey.

They allow us into the intimate thoughts of the partner of an addict, and the addict as well.

Reading about the struggles they had growing up and learning about Tim's heroin addiction was a shocking reminder and gave me a real sense of what can happen to someone caught in the vicious cycle of addiction. Picturing him standing in a hardware store doing returns for quick cash or renting furniture just to sell it to the dope man!

When we are in active addiction we may love somebody, we may care for someone deeply and even act that way or say so much, but ultimately the drugs are the only thing we really care about. We, as addicts, only focus on the ways and means of getting more drugs and everything else falls away.

I think the thing that most resonated with me is hearing how this affected Dr. Cali, how through Tim's addiction she was constantly challenged and fighting to get her Tim back, the Tim she had fallen in love with.

Relationships are hard but dealing with addiction will push anyone close to falling off the edge.

I myself had put my wife and family through this so many times, which is incredible to think about now. Reading about Tim and Dr. Cali's rough ride makes me even more grateful to be in my recovery, helping others.

Unfortunately, many addiction stories don't have a happy ending, but this one does, and it shows that the battle is worth it, we can win. If we do get clean, we recover ourselves, our lives, and even the ones we love.

Matt Bradley
Discovery Channel's *Deadliest Catch* and recovering addict

PROLOGUE

Tap, tap... tap, tap.

I feel like I'm drowning, smothered, and something is keeping me under. I suck in some air and try to clear my thinking.

Bang, bang, bang!

Air, I need more air, and to figure out who is making that fucking racket!

I finally lift my head, look over and there's a cop looking back at me, pounding on my car window and telling me, "Wake up sleepy head and roll down your window."

I flail a little as I figure out how to roll the window down and as it slides down, he says, "Guy behind you called. He reported you've been here awhile, says you sat through three green lights before he called. And that was some time ago. What're you doing snoozing in the middle of an intersection, at a red light? Where's the dope? Where's your heroin, bud?"

I blink a couple times with my mouth hanging open a little. I'm starting to come out of my underwater world, feeling a little less like my mind is wading through molasses.

"Huh? Dope? I...I'm f...fine, man. Just a little tired," I stammer.

My thinking is starting to speed up, getting jumpstarted by the conversation I am having with the Man in Blue. How the hell did I fucking nod out at the light? And keep my foot on the brake?

Panicking some as the thought of the bags of heroin stashed in the car enter my clouded consciousness, I blurt out, "No, no...man. No heroin, I'm just really tired. I swear."

"You're sleeping at the red light because you're tired? Right," he says. "Outta the car."

Just then the paramedics show up, strip off my shirt and stick those little electrodes all over my chest, so they can read my vital signs. I guess I check out as being alive and having some decent vitals, and the cop stuffs me in the back of his car. He turns and starts chatting with the medics.

I can barely make out what they're saying but can see his lips and I can tell he's asking if I'm on heroin. The paramedic says he can't be sure, can't really tell, so I start to work on my story. They come back over to the car and yank open the door.

"C'mon man, we know you're on something. Tell us what's going on, what drugs you're taking so we can help you, we don't want you to die at a red light," says the medic.

"I think I might be diabetic, it runs in my family," I lie.

"You're diabetic? You think, or you've been diagnosed?"

"I don't know, I've never been diagnosed. But my brother and my mother are both diabetic and they pass out all the time," I continue.

They shut the door again and I can see them talking some more, and the medic telling the cop I could be diabetic or just bullshitting, he doesn't know. They start to pack up their gear and load their rig to leave.

The cop watches them for a bit, pondering. I know he doesn't want to haul in another junkie and fill his afternoon with paperwork and sitting at a desk. He'd rather drive around in his car, drink coffee and hope for something more exciting to happen. Or for nothing at all to happen.

He opens the door and stares at me for a minute. I stare back, a little bleary-eyed, but the adrenaline if flowing a little now and kicking me back out of my nod.

He inquires slowly, "Do you think you can get this car home without fucking killing anyone?"

"Yes, yes sir."

He pulls me out, turns away and gets in the driver's seat, quickly pulling away and leaving me standing there amazed and a bit dumbfounded. He let me go, incredible.

The excitement of my surviving a near-incarceration and near-death experience leaves me feeling giddy, almost celebratory. I jump in the car and drive home. I love driving, going fast and feeling the power of the car. When I get home, I greet Cali with a kiss and act like everything is perfectly right in the world.

I jump in the shower, I'm a fucking mess, that cop had me sweating big time and I feel gnarly. While soaping up I notice one of those electrode things is still stuck to my chest. I barely remember the medics ripping them off, but man, I can't believe this one's still there.

If Cali would've seen that I would have had some major explaining to do and she would have seen through any bullshit lies I tried on her. I would've been done, I'm sure of it, out the door.

But she didn't see it, thankfully.

So, I'm not done yet, far from it.

PART I

GROWING UP IN THE AMERICAN DREAM

"I have spent my life judging the distance between American reality and the American Dream."
~ Bruce Springsteen

Cali

I was born in Pottstown, Pennsylvania which is basically a ghetto about forty minutes west of Philadelphia. There's not much to see or do as a kid and we hung out on the iconic High Street, racing cars, and blasting 80's hair band music.

I fell in love with Tommy Lee from Mötley Crüe when I was 14 and told myself, "Cali, someday you're going to marry that guy." The eyeliner, the spandex, the hair, I loved that hair. I have always liked the bad boys, their air of mystery and fun, the tattoos, fast cars, criminal records, all that shit really turned me on. My little ghetto world was so damn boring, and the wild, rocker lifestyle attracted me.

I have no fond memories of my childhood. I wish I had a few, but I really don't. My Mom made minimum wage at a job she had since her teen years and we were pretty much broke all the time, eating frozen TV dinners, hot dogs and shit-on-a-shingle for supper.

My Dad was a total hustler. He ran a car dealership, a gas station, a gun shop, a real estate office, a bunch of "businesses" where he "sold" people shit and scammed them out of their money.

But he never brought the cash home for us, it always went to whomever his current chick of the day was and there were a lot of them. Each one younger than the one before and his second wife was only a few years older than me. He expected me to call her mom and that did not go over so well.

There was always lots of yelling and anger. My father would call me fat, stupid, ugly and berate me all the time. Nice guy.

One time he said to my mother when she was dropping me at his place, "You're going grocery shopping? Don't bother! She is fat. She doesn't need to eat".

I was 13 at the time and it really fucking hurt, probably helped fuel my eating disorder and food addiction which led to my pill addiction. How many other little girls are subjected to this crap? Way too many, I'm afraid.

My mother chose to ignore it, or she was so traumatized by the constant hell of our life that she couldn't fix it. Either way, it went on daily. Mostly mental and emotional abuse, but there was some physical shit too. My jaw is permanently fucked up from an incident where my father jacked me against the refrigerator when I was 12.

"Do you want one of these candied apples," I asked. The next thing I knew, I was getting slammed into the corner of the fridge, my mouth connecting forcefully with the hard, cold metal. There were only three of the apples and he was mad about something, again. About the apples, about life, about me bugging him, who knows, really. He was just frustrated with life and I was his convenient punching bag.

Good Old Dad was diagnosed schizophrenic, but I realized later that was the wrong diagnosis. He is severely manic and bipolar. I used to get nervous before he got home, you never knew what was coming in the front door, everything from happy and laughing to sad and depressed. The worst was the screaming and angry Dad.

Sometimes he would give me his favorite record and I would save it in my special box of 45's. Then a week later he would accuse me of stealing it and spank me. And when I was eight, he emptied my bank account, every single penny of the $201.08 I had saved. I remember that exact amount because I had saved every birthday gift, every Christmas gift, every cent I had scrounged from the sidewalk. I was proud of my little bank account, it wasn't much but it was a start.

I was saving for college, I knew that could be my ticket out of this little corner of hell. No one had been to college in my family and I was told at an early age, "If you want something, then get a job." My dad and my grandmother never even graduated from high school and I knew at that age that I didn't fit with them and wanted to better myself.

My father stealing from me was far from the worst his sick mind could come up with, he used to play Russian Roulette with me. No shit, he would load the gun and put it to my head.

Click.

He taught me the trick to "winning" while playing this truly insane game. The bullet is heavy and sinks to the bottom as you spin the revolver's cylinder, so your first shot is never a kill shot. Never? Good to know, I guess, but I wouldn't bet my life on it.

Yeah, totally fucked up, living the nightmare not living the dream, that's for sure.

Tim

I had the great American childhood, typical "Leave It To Beaver" family life. My parents were both teachers and they were together until my Dad passed in 2016, a total of 57 years of marital bliss. My folks took care of us kids, I'm the middle of three boys, and our life was very orderly, predictably pleasant and comfortable. No drama, no trauma.

My older brother has worked for NASA and my younger brother is a school psychologist. Good family.

I was born and raised on the Space Coast of central Florida, which is Brevard County, and which is probably why my older brother ended working for NASA. I was born in Melbourne but when I was a few months old my parents moved us up to Titusville where I stayed until I was 17 years old.

Titusville, Florida was an extreme blue-collar town, which grew to support the NASA Space Center and the

Apollo missions in the 60s and 70s, and the space shuttle missions throughout the 80s and 90s. Lots of hard-working, patriotic families living a respectable life in a tropical paradise.

The economy was really booming, and things were exciting. The "race to the moon" with the rest of the world during the Apollo years was something everyone was proud to be a part of and it made everyone feel like fucking superstars when we won. The Shuttle missions kept the vibe strong and the money flowing too, life couldn't have been better.

During my childhood, Titusville was made up mostly of young families and lively. The streets were teeming with kids constantly playing outdoors, games like stickball or Marco Polo, good healthy, fun stuff. It was just 7 miles to Playa Linda Beach, which is the last all-natural beach on the central Florida coastline. Playa Linda means "beautiful beach" in Spanish, and I gotta admit, it is damn nice. I spent a lot of time surfing and just enjoying the seclusion and serenity, listening to the waves and feeling the sand between my toes.

Titusville was pretty much "Small Town, USA" and had the small-town mentality that went with the label. You know, the one where everybody basically knew everybody, and people watched out for their neighbors and gossiped with them too. The town also had all kinds of recreation programs for us kids, like baseball, basketball, and football. I joined all of them and was, essentially, outside playing in the sun my entire childhood. I was pretty much a sun-kissed, blessed American Boy.

However, it hasn't all been cookies and cream for Titusville, or me as well.

The city today is a very different place since the space program is closed and consequently, businesses have closed their doors. Families moved on to better economic situations, heading to other cities and states. When I go back now, I get the feeling that it's like a ghost town. There are no more kids, no more trick-or-treating on the streets for Halloween, no more sports programs, no more movie theaters. Even the mall has closed. That theme song from "The Good, The Bad, and The Ugly" always whistles through my head when I'm driving around, looking at the deserted landscape.

And in the 80s, the cocaine and crack epidemic ripped the city apart and I got caught up right in the middle of it.

I got into music when I was eight or nine years old, good hard-rockin' and guitar band shit. My cousin and I would put on makeup like Kiss, taking the time and effort to duplicate it just right, including a little fake blood now and then. Then we would pull out our fake instruments and put on these air band concerts on my cousin's back porch. We were so fucking cool.

When I was eleven, my mom bought me an acoustic guitar and it turned out I was pretty good at guitar but was horrible at singing. I totally sucked, my voice was all crackling, my rhythm on the guitar would get all thrown out of whack, and I couldn't hold a tune for shit.

I took band class in seventh grade, figuring I could get an easy good grade and I ended up playing the snare drum. I wasn't bad and I got my first drum set when I was fourteen. I was stoked, and it was totally on after that, I couldn't get enough of the loud, head-banging, metal music that would fuel my drumming sessions.

I was fourteen when I scored that first set of drums and that's when I also got involved with drugs. At the beginning, it was smoking weed and drinking alcohol with my buddies, classic teenager shit, just getting high for something to do and it all went perfect with my new rocker lifestyle, right? Then, when I was seventeen, I was introduced to cocaine and quickly switched to it and there was no turning back, damn I loved that coke.

What I didn't realize until I met Cali, was that I have severe A.D.D. and I need to be stimulated all the time. I remember saying, as a kid, that I was always bored. And guess what? Cocaine is pretty much the same thing as Adderall. Without knowing it, I was self-medicating with my newly discovered coke habit and life was cruising right along with everything just hunky dory.

Cali

My dad used to keep guns in the basement and he taught me how to shoot. He also got me to learn how to drive a go-kart. In some ways, I'm more of a boy than a girl. I can't cook or clean, but I can change oil and drive a stick shift. I don't much care for diamonds and the only bling you see on me is my Jeep rims. I am different like that, mostly rough and a lot of tumble.

My father wanted a boy. One time, I dropped a brick on my foot helping him build the garage and it swelled up like a balloon.

He told me, "Suck it up Buttercup, ice it and get back to work!"

I ended up at the Emergency Room later in the day when my mom's friend saw my foot and forced him to take me to the hospital.

Then he wanted to be all Billy Badass and race there with his yellow construction light flashing, like the savior. He had a buddy who was a cop, so he even organized a police escort. It was a shit show, and as always, he made it all about him.

I knew my dad was cheating on my mom way before she would ever acknowledge it. The worst part was her so-called “best friend” knew too and didn't tell her. That must suck.

How does your husband cheat on you with half the town and you just pretend it is not happening? I don't think I could do that.

I told my mom, “You’re either going to divorce him or I’m going to put a bullet in his brain. He’s cheating on you with everybody. Those are your two options.”

So, she sent me to a counselor. That was her answer.

That was my first experience with some sort of therapist and I lasted a whole twenty minutes before I got kicked out of her office.

She had handed me a coloring book and asked, “Why don’t you color your feelings?” I tore it in half and promptly told her, “Go fuck herself.”

She immediately deposited me in the waiting room, stating, “This child is too aggressive and inappropriate.” So, my mother took me home and that was that.

After my mother and father divorced, my mother called her sister. They decided it was a “good idea” for her and her husband and their three kids to all move in with us. Eight people jammed into a cramped, claustrophobic, and stinky three-bedroom house. There was mold in basement and old wiring. The house rules included; no flushing every time you peed and no using more than one towel. After all, water was not cheap.

Good idea, right.

My Aunt's husband, I guess technically he was my uncle, was a mean, nasty son of a bitch and bossed me around like I was his property or something. My aunt called me names like "Miss Piggy" because I was chubby.

Two of her kids were no nicer to me. The middle boy called me names and would steal my things and hide them in the neighbor's yards. One day her daughter and I got into it like a couple of all-star wrestlers. I put my hand through the glass door and that got their attention. Of course, everyone blamed me, and I was labeled "The Wild Child."

My mother is very naïve and clueless, just one of those people who doesn't want to be bothered by reality sometimes.

She's always "blinders on," doesn't pay attention or know anything's happening. So, she ignored household dysfunction and abuse for thirteen years. She ignores pretty much anything in life that is confrontational, and she hates to argue, avoids it like the plague. She likes to garden, so peaceful and Zen.

Tim

"Your Dad wants to come pick to us up and take us out to eat."

My girlfriend at the time I was 17, Rebecca, told me this and it did not really compute. My Dad? That's weird, I remember thinking. I hadn't talked to my Dad in a couple of weeks. Our relationship had cooled after I started really playing music and dropping out of sports. He really wanted me to become a baseball player, he thought I had the talent if I could just apply myself.

I climbed into the car and Rebecca hopped in the backseat, behind me.

"Hey Dad, how's it going?"

"Tell me about your cocaine problem," he said, flatly.

My heart sank. I glanced over the seat and Rebecca was looking down, picking her fingernails nervously. I know she'd told him about my drug use, she'd been worried and telling me to cool it some.

"No way, I'm not using cocaine, that's crazy!" I insisted.

He knew I was lying and just gave me a look, a look that said, "I'm so hurt."

It would have almost been better if he just yelled at me, but he didn't. We went out to eat and afterward, when he dropped us off, I just looked at the ground and mumbled, "Sorry."

It didn't cut it, I know. He was at a loss and didn't know what to do with me. And I had no idea how to talk to him either.

He was a school principal and dealt with all kinds of bad apples, kids with problem lives and problem parents. He was very respected in our area and if there were schools struggling with the bad kids and the bad grades, the superintendent sent my Dad in there to turn the school around.

So, he had a reputation for being a tough guy and you didn't fuck around in my dad's schools. Well, you know, I heard it got out that his son was a cocaine user, and people used that against him. It really put a hurting on his career and that's one thing I carry a lot of guilt around over.

I heard he was in an expulsion meeting with all his peers and superintendent and, of course, the troubled kid and their parent were there.

My Dad's there trying to expel this kid, and then the parent screams out, "Oh, yeah! Well, you know your son's a cocaine addict, you know. What gives you the right to be in charge of my kid? What do you know?!"

He sheepishly tried with me, to reach me somehow and understand my drug use for a couple years. Then he backed down. He was always a great Dad, would give you the shirt off his back and anything you needed. But, it started to feel like it was one of those deals, where either I'm going to get myself squared away...or kill myself. And he knows there's not much he can do about it.

Cali

I should have been a hardcore drug addict in my teens. I should have been a bad kid, getting into trouble all the time, but I became a survivor. I learned to toughen up and push through the hard shit. I didn't numb out, instead, I learned from them, from all the crazy behaviors and became motivated by them.

I used to throw talent shows with the neighbor kids and charge the parents to get in. I would bake and sell my cookies and cakes. I even created a newsletter and sold that.

All that cash was added to my growing college fund. I was going to go, get out of Dodge and make it big, dammit.

I was into being an entrepreneur. I guess I got that from my Dad, which is one of the few nice things I can say about the guy.

Cali

I lived in my hometown until I was nineteen and then I split. Stowe girls, as we called ourselves were resilient. A lot of us overcame some serious hardships just to survive. At 19, I was done 'just surviving'. I packed everything I owned in my 1974 CJ7 Jeep and moved the hell out of there. I headed to Penn State and got myself a Bachelor's in psychology.

One night, my roommate came home at 2 am and I was on the floor eating cake with my hands.

There was cake on the dog, cake on the walls, cake on the floor. Cake was matted into my hair.

And I was crying. I was miserable.

Always the girl that went out and came home alone when my roommates would hook up with guys. All I could hear in my head were those words drilled into me as a girl, by my father and others, "You are fat and ugly."

I went to the see the counselor at school and she said I didn't get the official Diagnostic and Statistical Manual of Mental Disorders (DSM) diagnosis for an eating disorder because I would eat and not vomit.

I had learned that trick from my mom.

My grandmother would bake and have all the women over to eat cake and drink coffee. After they left, and everyone went to bed, my mother would get me and sneak down, and we would eat cake.

All of it.

I learned you eat cake when you are stressed. You eat cake when you are happy, you eat cake to celebrate. You eat cake when you are sad. Cake is the answer to all your issues. The more cake the better.

I was a junkie. A food junkie.

But I didn't fit the DSM criteria because back in the 1990s there was no such thing. People with eating disorders either didn't eat or ate and threw up. I did neither, so I simply didn't fit their eating disorder model. I just liked cake and had a hard time controlling my sugar cravings.

While I was studying psychology at Penn State University, I ended up in an addiction class and I felt strangely at home. I related to what was being discussed, yet I wasn't using drugs or alcohol to excess. I mean I drank here and there like all college kids, but I have been drunk only twice in my life. Not really my thing to be out of control, sloppy all over the place. I like to be in control of myself, my thinking. But food and sugar, once I get going, it can be hard to stop, like a runaway train.

While at PSU, I got the opportunity to intern at SCI Rockview, a medium-security male prison right up the street from the juvenile detention center where I was working at the whopping rate of $7.00 per hour. I jumped at the chance to work in a real prison, I couldn't wait to work with all the crazy behaviors and sex offenders! A budding psychologist's dream come true!

But no, they put me on the "light detail" and I got to work with the drug and alcohol offenders. Guys in for DUI, weed possession, drug trafficking offenses. I really had no interest in it, these guys are "small time," I thought. I wanted to work with the sex offenders, but my mentor made me work the addicts. Bring on the rapists, right!? That sounded interesting.

I thought it would be boring working with a bunch of drunks and stoners.

I was wrong, dead wrong. It was fascinating, and I learned so much in five months of interning full-time for no pay. It was probably the most exciting job I have ever had, and I learned how to run groups and make it fun. I learned how to sit across from a psychopath and have zero fear. I even had to be alone in a cell with these guys while the Penn state shooter of 1995 was loose on campus and they locked us down for hours.

I learned how to read body language extremely well and to understand that what was said verbally, was not always what someone really meant. I learned the criminal code. I learned how the staff is often sicker and worse than the clients and I watched staff smuggle in drugs and sleep with the inmates. It was probably the most intense and impactful learning experience of my higher education.

I liked the addicts. I got along with them, I understood them, and felt like they were my people.

Back on campus, the school counselor didn't know what to do with me because I didn't fit the eating disorder profile in the DSM. And apparently, I didn't fit the addict profile in there either.

She says, "I'm referring you to the doctor." She didn't know what to do with my issue, my unnamed food addiction.

So, I must just be fat.

The doctor recommended diet pills and it turned out I loved those. Legal speed.

Excellent! Now I can eat all the cake and pizza I want and pop a few pills and lose weight.

Oh yes, this was the perfect solution. That counselor, it's amazing that she was so smart in referring me.

Let's not solve the problem of why I eat to cover my emotions, just give me some good old big pharma nonsense drugs so I can still eat to cover my emotions but look sexy doing it.

Within 3 months, I was a whopping 90 pounds soaking wet. And at 5'2" tall I did look anorexic.

I came home from college and my mother was horrified. "Are you a drug addict? Are you doing crack cocaine?"

"No Mom, they're legal...legal diet pills."

After about a year of living on my modified diet of bad food, lots of exercise, and those fantastic diet pills the heart palpitations started, then panic attacks.

I went to a different doctor, and he says, “What are you on?”

“On? I’m not ‘on’ anything. Nothing.”

He raised an eyebrow, listened to my heart. He said it had a murmur, sounded like there was something going on, something not quite right.

“It seems to me like you’re on some sort of stimulant. Speed? Diet Pills??

I lied, “Nope, not here.”

I left my easily-persuaded doctor and headed back to the gym, the cake, the diet pills and the panic attacks, which got progressively worse. The heart and chest pain were so severe at times, that I almost checked myself into in the ER.

I did go back to the doctor, a different guy, and this time I was seen by a cardiologist, sure that I was having some sort of heart attack or heart valve issue. This guy knew instantly what was going on. He lectured me, “No pills. No speed. No caffeine!”

I tried to listen to him and cut out the pills, as a result, I detoxed, hard.

Alone an on the floor for days. It was bad. I was tired, lethargic and eating cake again with no happy magic pills to quash the cravings.

Its 4 am all over again and it’s déjà vu. I am crying, eating cake. There’s cake on the walls, cake on the dog, cake on the floor. Somehow, I suffer through and I can ditch the diet pills.

I get sober, just white-knuckled through it and then headed back to see the counselor.

I ask, "Now what?"

Within 10 minutes, I am out the door with a Narcotics Anonymous pamphlet and an Overeaters Anonymous Pamphlet.

Off to my first OA meeting I went, held in the classic dark Church basement. It's gray and winter and fucking cold. There's no coffee, which I find weird, no sugar, which makes sense, and no smokes. This trip to The Rooms is full of complaining, bitter individuals, and completely void of help. Frustrated with the experience, I left to try NA, maybe it would be better.

Same dingy, dark basement, same unhappy, frustrated addicts battling their demons. But wait, there's one extremely notable exception. Candy, donuts, and coffee by the truckload!

All the coffee and sugar I can handle and smokes too, sweet...

Wait a minute, I can eat doughnuts but don't touch the cocaine. Which I didn't get because the rule was no mind-altering substances. But sugar? It was a major mind-blowing substance for me, for anyone, really. And sugar, I had come to realize, was my major drug of choice. Not just refined sugar, but simple carbohydrates like stuff made with flour. Pasta, bread, all those home-baked items I had grown up with, snacked on regularly and treasured.

I realized this NA shit was not going to work for me and I called a friend crying, "I don't know what to fucking do! I'm going crazy...I gotta find a way to stay off speed and not eat myself into a hippo!"

She simply responded, "Cali, I think I have something that will help. I've been hooked for a while now, and it is way better than any drug."

I'm grateful to this day for her introducing me to yoga.

That first time, I'll be honest, it sucked balls. I couldn't touch my toes and I couldn't reach the mat. Up, down, up, I was winded and grunting and damn, it *hurt*.

I made it through the hour, barely, and it helped the instructor was so nice. He invited me back, said, "Keep trying, don't give up. I know it's a bitch at first, but you'll get it. It'll be worth it, I guarantee it."

That sounded familiar...

My friend talked me into going back and dragged me to class. I cried at the end of it, a gentle sobbing, which I kept to myself. It was so hard, and I wasn't used to having my ass kicked like this.

Somehow, I managed to go again, and I learned something that I had never been able to do before.

I learned to let the mat have my anxieties. I could just push my stress, worry, grief, and anger into the mat, and leave it there.

I didn't need the fridge or the cake anymore, I had yoga. After twenty sun salutations, I didn't want the cake. I felt a peace wash over me, it was kind of blissful as the cravings for sugar slowly drifted away. I was able to break the connection of my desire to escape unhappy thoughts and feelings with food and replace it with breathing and movement.

Even though meetings didn't work for me, I knew they worked for others. I found myself wanting to get a deeper understanding and learn this new way of coping because I was sure that other people could benefit from my experience.

I fell in love with Yoga and I quickly became an Instructor. I wanted to have an inner core peace and serenity and teach it to others. I had replaced my cravings for sweets with a craving for mental health and physical fitness. I added Pilates and a Personal Training Certification along the way.

Now I knew how to eat, what to eat and when to eat. I had known all along that food fuels the body, but I had an enormous appreciation for the intricacies of nutrition. I also realized that food is basically nourishment. It can be delicious and a fantastic experience, to enjoy healthy, gourmet cuisine. But, food is so often a reward, and in it seemed to me that we celebrate everything with a cake.

Having a wedding? Let's eat a gigantic, piece of frosting covered art.

Is it your birthday? When do you get to blow out the candles and eat your cake?

I've been to divorce parties where there is a cake shaped in the anatomy of the male for easy torture and destruction. (Sorry guys.)

Baby-shower? Yup, we have cake and cupcakes.

Cake is happy food, and for some, like me, it is an addiction.

It just wasn't in the DSM... yet.

My first job out of college was at a shelter for runaway girls. It was fun and rewarding teaching them how to be empowered, to take control of their situation and change it for the better because I always thought of myself as a survivor. And a lot of these girls struggled with addiction, which was quickly becoming my focus, my obsession.

I entered the addictions field with my head held high with my next gig when I got hired at a long-term treatment center for women with children. As you can imagine, it was loud, lots of talking and screaming and talking loudly to talk over the talking and screaming. Ugh, I was the working poor and it was hard to live on my meager paycheck with student loans and a car loan. Not to mention federal tax, state tax, city tax and breathing tax. Addictions treatment can be rewarding in a way, just not often in a financial way.

I was miserable.

Tim

"Thanks guys!" I told the delivery crew from Rent-A-Center as they were loading up the moving blankets and straps into the back of their truck.

"Cash fine for the payment?"

"Sure, I got your invoice right here Mr. Walker. You have exact change?" asked the driver.

I had ordered up an entire living room set, complete with two recliners, an entertainment center, a TV, end tables, lamps, a full-on giant sofa with a pull-out bed. The works.

And they only wanted the first month's rent paid up front.

I cashed them out and as soon as they left the vacant apartment I had commandeered for the afternoon, I started making calls.

"Mike? Yeah, it's me, Tim. The sale is on, let your guys know."

It wasn't long before pickup trucks and other vehicles started to arrive. Some were dealers I knew well, too well really. And we made deals for the furniture. Cash deals, drug deals, deals for future drug and cash deals.

By the time the sun was setting, all the cars and trucks were gone and so was the rented furniture.

In its place was a crap-load of cocaine, with plenty of it already up my nose. Along with a substantial wad of cash and the other future trades I was able to negotiate, I was totally set for a while.

And, with plenty of these stupid furniture rental morons out there and all kinds of vacant apartments to pick from, I could keep this sweet scam going indefinitely.

I was even getting it to work with jewelry rent-to-own places. Come on, really? Who rents jewelry to own and doesn't expect to get ripped off? I'm sure they have insurance for that stuff anyway.

Cali

The clients didn't want to be sober and the system didn't care if they made it or not, so I decided something had to change.

I felt I wanted to learn more and I needed to learn more. More knowledge meant more pay and a higher caliber of clientele. I wanted clients that wanted to see me, people who really desired a life change and understood that to reach the success they desired, having someone to help them find the right path was worth the extra expense. It was downright depressing working with those who were court ordered or were scamming the welfare system to stay high.

I set out on a quest to learn as much as I could, and I studied Psychodrama, Energy Work, Reiki, and more Yoga. I dove into Massage Therapy and Reflexology. I became a Personal Trainer and Life Coach. I researched and studied Designer Drugs, Positive Psychology, and fine-tuned my Motivational Interviewing skills. I was willing to become an expert at anything that interested me, and I set out to master almost anything related to addiction recovery.

I have no fewer than twenty-four certifications. I not only have all the standard training required by therapists in my field. but I am not just a "sit-behind-the-desk-and-ask-you-how-you-are-feeling" therapist. I am in your face, like a drill sergeant. I am a "get-it-fixed, now" coach. I like results, I get them, and my clients get them too.

I went on to get my Master's Degree in Criminal Justice while focusing on studying the Addicted Personality at West Chester University. I wanted to fully understand why addicts engage in criminal activity and innovate ways I can help fix the broken system.

I focused on my specialty there, which is Cognitive Behavioral Therapy and Therapeutic Community, a common prison-style approach of "Break 'em Down Then Build 'em Up." My friends, colleagues, and clients would not describe me as warm and fluffy. Being a bit of a full-on hard ass is exactly what some addicts need and it's exactly what they'll get with me.

I tell them, "I look forward to the day you fire me because that means I did my job."

I see mostly men because of my direct nature. I also connect with Type A women, and of course, I love my gays. They can handle sarcasm and don't mind getting teased a little. If you have a nanny, a personal trainer, no job and you are "stressed out," I am not the coach for you because I will simply tell you to put your big girl panties on and suck it up buttercup.

Most women hate that. Men love it. Thanks Dad for the tips, they have come in handy.

My style is unique, and I get to the root cause of the issue fast and furious. There's no time or reason to mess around and I start working to help the client fix their issues and create goals and objectives. I blend forward progressive psychology, with coaching, which is forward progressive movement. The movement, or actions, includes combining nutrition, yoga, and exercise with vitamin therapy and cutting-edge nutraceuticals that cross the blood-brain barrier and restore the brain pathways.

I put all that together and it makes me a powerhouse, a force to be reckoned with, which forces many addicts to finally make some progress. Most of my clients have tried over and over to get sober and stay sober and have failed miserably. Often it wasn't until they encountered someone who wouldn't pussyfoot around their issues that they finally got it and found a way out of their turmoil.

I managed to piss off many of my colleagues early on, and they loved to create a lot of drama. I got gallons of nasty "Hateraid" on social media. None of it true so I had to wait it out and hope they would eventually get bored and find something more productive to do, like save lives.

The addiction industry is one of the nastiest, cutthroat industries you will ever encounter. You have your average run-of-the-mill shady stuff but then you have these inner circles of people that do not want to be infiltrated, almost like the mafia. They fear you will somehow take their clients or move in on their segment of the market. These people had the industry on lockdown, and it was mostly these undereducated interventionists and their untrained instructors that feared me coming into "their space" and trying to raise the bar on education.

There was a genuine distrust of any changes to their system they had created and to me, it felt like they despised some good old-fashioned competition.

I have always said there are people that are clean and sober and then there are those in recovery. In the addictions recovery field, it's occasionally said that the therapist is sicker than the client. Sometimes that is very true.

Over the next 20 years, I would often be forced to weather the storm and I would learn that is not what you know, but who is contained in your trusted circle.

I would buck the system all the way and I would create my own circle.

But first I would take a break from the infighting and industry-wide backstabbing.

Tim

I was thinking, "I'm really rocking out here! This band is actually good, man!"

I'm playing drums, hammering away with a blues band and it's a full house, like 500 strong. But I also remember feeling, "It's kind of weird, playing for all these guys, no girls."

I'm in a prison yard, Marion Correctional, and this was as good as it could get. Prison is no cakewalk and this gig with the blues band was dreamed up to keep morale out of the gutter. I was lucky to know how to drum and get a spot.

I was in the middle of a four-and-a-half-year stint for that sweet rent-to-own scam I was pulling. They finally caught up with me and I couldn't believe I got busted.

Next time around I got sentenced to two years for possession of cocaine, and ecstasy, love that stuff. As part of my sentence, I got to go to inpatient rehab for six months. I wasn't looking to get sober or anything, but I thought it would be better than prison.

The rehab, Bridges of America, was started by Frank Constantino who was released from prison, in Florida, and as an ex-felon out on parole, experienced a spiritual awakening. As a result, he opened his first outpatient treatment facility, and I had the great fortune to land there.

Frank was an ex-mafia gangster and he had a bunch of rehabs all over the state of Florida, I was supposed to go to the one in Orlando for six months. Actually, I was there for seven months because I got caught with Hydroxycut, which is a stimulant, and they gave me 30 extra days because they thought I was using it to get high.

I was only using it to cut body fat, while I was on a strict workout regimen. I was trying to put on some muscle and lean out a little bit, but they didn't see it that way.

I was sent to rehab because my cocaine habit had started to cause me all kinds of problems, legal and personal. I was just hoping to figure out a way to get through the rehab deal, I don't think I really intended to quit. Quitters never win.

One of my good friends at the rehab was in there for heroin and he went home on one of these furloughs.

He got back and showed me the stash he smuggled back in, "You want a taste?"

"No way man, not my thing," I said.

They found him dead in the bathroom the following morning. He went in there and shot up and he had been clean for so long. I'm sure he shot at the same amount that he was doing back in the day.

As they say, addicts are going to wind up in one of three places: Prison, the Morgue, or Recovery. Drugs will get you to do some crazy shit sometimes, and let you believe you are somehow invincible. By the end of my drug-fueled crime spree several years ago, I had racked up no fewer than 24 felonies and 14 misdemeanors, all drug-related.

I'm here to testify, "It's not like the game, that's for sure."

Although I remember it getting a little too real, playing that game. I was back home, in Titusville.

I was working a street deal, trying to score and the dude jumps in the car, pulls a gun, and stuffs it into my ribcage.

"Drive motherfucker!" he screams.

I kind of froze for a second, not knowing what to do, just dazed and wondering, "Is this really happening?"

He yells again, "Drive, dumbass, drive!"

I started slowly driving, made it about 200 yards and just jammed the car into park. I jumped out, expecting to hear a gunshot or feel a bullet rip into me any second. Time was moving in slow motion. I felt like I was trying to move through quicksand.

I hauled ass as fast as I could and the wacko with the gun just got behind the wheel and tore off.

The police found my car the next day and I made up some bullshit story about it getting stolen in the grocery store parking lot when I was inside.

PART II

LIVING THE DREAM

"You want to live the dream?
You do what you want on your terms."
~ Courtney Love

Cali

I hate the Pennsylvania winters and I am sure 99.999% of the people stuck in Pennsylvania agree with me. I mean, it's cold, damp, dark, and icy. It's so damn dreary, those gray skies, the gray snow, the pale depressed people, all bored to tears like me.

Yuck.

Give me some palm trees and sunshine. Give me fresh mangos and pineapples. Give me shorts in February and being surrounded by happiness and faces smiling back at me.

I yearned to be warm year-round and to enjoy life.

I told one of the guys I was working with, "I gotta get out of this place, it's like everyone is in mourning or something, it's just not good for my soul. I really want to go to California, somewhere warm and upbeat."

"Texas is cheap and warm," he said. "And everything's bigger in Texas," he went on.

"Maybe I'll check it out. I need something, a change, some sun, something. I'm going fucking bonkers here."

So, I packed everything I owned into my Explorer, including my giant, 100-pound malamute, and moved to Texas.

My friend was spot on. I had central AC for the first time in my life.

That guy, Alan, and I ended up starting a fitness company with no money, just my crappy Walmart computer, not even a desk.

I turned a plastic clothing bin upside and sat on the floor for the first six months.

I sacrificed it all and just worked with what I had, which wasn't much. But I was determined to make it, there was no going back to the dismal world I had come from. I needed to find a way to succeed.

I took out loans on my personal credit cards for business cards, rent, pay per click marketing, all of it. I simply financed all of it at extremely high-interest rates, but I believed.

I wanted to make something huge and help people improve their own world, their life somehow. That felt good to me and I loved the happy clients who enjoyed the positive transformation.

At the time, there just was not much addiction treatment going on in Dallas. As a bodybuilder with tons of local connections, Alan knew the fitness industry inside and out. I had always been a great student, I listened, and I learned. I tapped into my experiences on the yoga mat and together we created a rapidly growing, exciting organization.

We built the largest in-home personal training company in the nation. We did some things wrong, no doubt about it, but we did some things right and the company hit $4.1 million in its third year. We had four offices, over 1,000 independent contractors and 17 in-house staff. We had a penthouse in Downtown Dallas which had us feeling on top of the world.

We told each other, "We're making it! Hell, yeah!"

I pulled 15-hour days, my obsessive side helping me to focus on the business only and it felt exhausting but exhilarating at the same time.

Then, as quickly as it came, we lost it all during the economic downturn of 2008. One of the first things to go during the recession is your personal trainer if you have one. If you can't pay the mortgage, you're not going to keep a trainer, completely disposable.

Overnight. Gone. Poof.

I was able to pay all but a handful of staff and almost every client got their money back while we shut down our offices across the country. It sucked putting these people out of work, the amazing fitness family we had grown. It was just no longer an option.

Tim

"There is absolutely nothing out here," I was thinking as our beat-down shit-ride of a van barreled across West Texas on our way to New Mexico for the night.

My band, The Deadlyz, and I were on our way to L.A. from a Dallas gig and sure we were going to be the next Mötley Crüe, we had it goin' on.

Well, there was something out there, fucking cops, bored as shit looking for something, anything, or anyone to hassle and hopefully bust for whatever weak charge they could pin on them.

And they were on our tail, right now, lights flashing and pulling our tour van over.

"You know your headlights aren't on? It's pretty much dark, you can't be driving around like that," the Sherriff's deputy from Podunkville informed us.

"Really? They were working last night...I had 'em on I thought..."

"Sure, right. License and registration please."

I reach over and grab the registration from my co-pilot, our bleary-eyed guitarist who was smoking a cigarette and trying not to look too scared. We had plenty of weed on board, not to mention our bass player in the back, a highly illegal migrant from Brazil. He sort of came in legally and just never left. Not exactly a favorite of the Texas law enforcement community.

I handed over the paperwork and my license to the officer and stayed quiet, just waiting.

"Can you explain this? And I need to see your registration."

"Wh..what? That is the registration, isn't it?"

We had been joking around when we created our tour itinerary and had written all kinds of funny "stops" along the way.

Mr. officer read it out loud.

"Guns, drugs, whores, cocaine." He stopped and looked up at me. Our Tour Itinerary was in the glove box with the registration and that's what our guitar player had handed out to the state troopers.

"Oh, ah...yeah...that's just a joke!" I tried to explain.

They had us all bail out of the van while they searched it for the guns and drugs. Obviously, we had no hookers on board, but they truly thought we some sort of cartel or something.

They searched through our equipment and came up empty-handed. Thankfully, our illegal had managed to quickly consume the last of our weed stash before we had to hop out of the van. We were pissed later when we laughed about it, though, while he was all stoned and zoned.

The cops let us go and we ambled on to the next little town, probably theirs, where we could crash for the night since our headlights were out. After that, we made sure to only travel during the day.

When we got to L.A. we didn't have any money, so we went to the Dollar Store and bought plenty of cheap wine and got drunk. The lead singer and I got in a fight.

The tour had been falling apart, our shows weren't what we had thought they would be. Mötley Crüe, my ass.

We got into a big knock-down drag-out brawl in the middle of Sunset Strip, screaming at each other and gathering quite the crowd.

TMZ came running up to film because they thought we were somebody they wanted to see. They thought they were getting some hot footage, but it wasn't long until they realized we were nobody. The crew walked away but they had come running up to film. It was exciting and depressing at the same time.

We were stars for a second, before the TMZ guys realized we were just another bunch of drunk and desperate musicians, a dime-a-dozen in L.A.

Cali

I moved out to Los Angles for a little while and started looking for a job. I loved L.A. and Laguna Beach was my spot. But it's expensive, there was no work, and I was running out of what money I had left from my Texas business melt-down.

I had to get back into the addictions industry and I was trying to avoid it because it was grueling and unlike fitness, your clients don't want to see you. Long hours for little pay and little joy isn't very appealing, even when your broke ass is trying to scrape enough cash together for a burrito.

I ended up heading back to Philly, tail between my legs and needing to hit the reset button. With no job, no income, and no savings I was hunkered down in a house with no running water and no heat. It was me, my dog, my laptop, and my gym bag sharing our combined warmth during a dismal Christmas season.

My clothes, furniture, and anything else of value were on the way to me in a moving truck. It wasn't much, but it was all I had left after my rise and fall on the business battlefield. Then the call came, all my items had burnt up in a warehouse fire or something, the details were pretty sketchy. Two weeks later the moving company dumped my charred, stinking items on the front lawn. They had no insurance and I didn't either, a total loss. The fake moving company I hired had stolen the identity of another company and no one could find them to collect on the damages or anything.

I had no job, no money, no clothes, and no furniture all while surrounded by the constant Pennsylvania gloom. Life was horrible. It was Christmas in PA and I had nothing.

I finagled a gym membership and spent my days there, working out, going to yoga and cleaning up.

And Wawa had refillable coffee for 90 cents. Between my one coffee and one sandwich a day I got by while trying to remain upbeat about my future and not dwelling on the past.

I applied for jobs and watched my credit go to hell when I couldn't make my Jeep payment and the bills piled up. I was feeling helpless and not one soul stepped up to help me. My business partner disappeared and left me to take the continued fallout from our failed venture.

This was the lesson of the "Safety Net" I learned. I had up until this point felt that the world owed me for my crappy childhood, that when times get tough someone would be there to catch you when you fell. But when I lost everything, I learned a hard lesson: The world owes you nothing.

No one owes you anything and no one must step up to help you. I learned how to fly without a safety net and material stuff was not important anymore. I had no things to be attached to and no support system to coddle me and get me back on my feet. I learned to do it on my own, sink or swim as they say.

I kept applying to jobs for the next three, depressing months while subsisting on my "no frills" budget and lifestyle. I had to, it was all I had. And the belief I would land one soon.

Later that winter, in Philly, with no money to go anywhere, I finally got a job. It was quite possibly the most horrendous employment experience of my life.

I found myself at a local psychiatric facility for children, answering a fucking phone all day long. I was so pissed off and frustrated. My title was the Admissions Coordinator, but I didn't coordinate anything. I answered the phone, I answered questions, and I certified insurance.

I was a glorified secretary with a Master's Degree. My last title was Owner/Founder/CFO, now I was answering the phone and I worked for peanuts. I was able to eat and pay for kerosene for my smelly heater, but that was it.

I wasted time by playing solitaire while working the quiet, boring second shift alone. I had a lot of time to think, to reflect, and to plan my escape.

I vowed, if the universe would give me another company, I would do it better and give away more money than I kept. That was my deal with the devil, or universe, as I call it. Please, just one more shot and get me the hell out of PA again.

I wasn't sure about seeing clients again, but it was better than the phone gig, so I started with just a few sessions here and there. It's high stress and exhausting to listen to people's problems all day long. But I was good at it, very good at it, and I made a difference in people's lives. A positive difference, at least for the few who were open to change. Hearing and seeing their success helped me feel good about what I was doing, even though the pay sucked.

I continued my struggle to pay the bills, the old student loan debt, and keep myself fed.

Then, when my business partner asked me what I'd do if I could do anything I thought, "Musicians aren't too bad."

"Let's start some sort of music industry related company," I said. "Let's help people that are excited to have us help them."

So, that's what we did.

Tim

"You know where you're goin?"

Johnny, our singer, had somehow got on the bridge and it did not look like it was the way we wanted to be going. It looked like we were on our way to Canada or something.

He had insisted on driving because he was from Detroit.

"I know this area," he had assured us.

And next thing we know, he accidentally drove us over the bridge into Canada. We were not prepared for that kind of crap and we totally got detained over there. Our bass player was illegal, and I have too many felonies. What the hell, we didn't want to go into Canada anyway.

"It was a mistake," we explained to the border agents, but that didn't faze them, they still made us go through customs, it was a nightmare.

After hours of waiting and questioning and reading my pages and pages of felonies that they printed, they finally let us just turn around and head back to the United States.

"Can you let us back in?"

Same shit, we had to explain why we were coming back into the United States. Somehow, we convinced them of our stupidity, maybe it didn't take much convincing. But the whole time we thought we were going to lose our bass player.

The guitar player, Burton disappeared after we got to Chicago. He's a sex addict and we couldn't find him for several hours.

"Where were you? I asked after he finally shows up.

And tells me his story, how he went down to the South Side of Chicago to score and got robbed.

"Yeah, bitch took my money," he confessed.

He's embarrassed and drops it. He's straight out of Brooklyn and he always did great with the women in New York. But when you leave New York, that's a different kind of look and accent and he had trouble with the ladies on tour. He was trying so hard, but every girl he hit on was not interested. The accent, the hair, too much gel, and no one really cares that you're in a rock band.

Cali

I met Tim shortly after his band, The Deadlyz, hired my new music marketing company. I was still in Philly but would go to New York to meet potential clients and was just getting to roll within the music industry. I took any client that stumbled through the door, and Tim was no exception.

I met him and his band at a Starbuck's in Manhattan and talked to them like I knew what I was doing and had been in the industry for years. I was good at that, talking and creating a connection, getting to know the band and acting like I had known them forever as friends.

They had found me online and were looking for help marketing and creating a buzz. I understood marketing and online presence, MySpace was just kicking off and ReverbNation hadn't been a household name yet, so our niche was a custom electronic press kit (EPK).

I got to tag along on some of their gigs for a couple months. One of the shows I went along to see was a festival in upstate New York, think Woodstock but more rock n' roll. One of the band members opens the van doors to get inside with a train of women behind him. It was like an orgy, or more like a parade: into the van, out of the van, in the van, out.

That went on for hours and it was a good education for me on sex addiction. The drugs flowed, the women stood in line (after all a few of these guys were semi-famous and had played with some big acts).

This was real rock n' roll.

They started to do a USA tour, Arizona, LA, Detroit, Chicago etc. I flew into Detroit to catch them at the iconic IROC and had a blast. Lots of guys from the 80s, still playing, still getting high.

I got to road dog, see how it is done, watch the guys in between shows, even watch one club owner try to pay them with cocaine, cheap beer, and food. THAT doesn't put gas in their tank to get to the next town.

They played the South Side of Chicago after Detroit. It was in the projects right on the border and we got there we were told, "You can stay in the basement. We have it set up down there so that bands can crash and sleep."

Part of the deal for the show was the included lodging and a meal, so I guess this is it. A dingy little basement for a dressing room.

And of course, we were supposed to get paid a percentage of the door and the bar when it came time to get paid.

We were there at 2:00 in the afternoon and they set up. We could order anything off the menu, had our dinner, then we hung out and walked around some before the band played. It was 2:00 o'clock in the morning and time to get paid, chill out for a little bit.

The owner of the joint came downstairs with this tray. Four guys in the band and he had four Blue Ribbon beers, real big ones one for each guy. And a whole mountain of cocaine.

And literally said, “Here you go!”

The guitar player, Burton, used to play for a band which had opened for Marilyn Manson. He was so excited.

“This is awesome!”

And the singer was the pretty much same way.

Well, the bass player didn't do hard drugs. He was extra careful about what kind of stuff he put in his body. He was way into his body and his image and how he looked, and he was pissed. He once shut the entire electric off at a show trying to flat iron his hair. He came upstairs and yelled ‘I can not go on stage with half a hair” in his broken English. Drugs, not him.

Tim was pissed.

He said, “Well that's not going to gas in our gas tank to get to the next show. How are we supposed to get from Chicago to the next show?”

They were going back to New York.

“That's not what we agreed upon. We agreed upon money.”

There was a big argument that went on for a half hour or more after Tim and the bass player Gabe refused to accept the coke as payment. Tim stormed upstairs to load the van and threw his big orange, flame-covered drum set down the steps. He was done, he was out of there.

Tim was furious that the club owner stiffed them on pay, and he ended up asking me to manage them and negotiate contracts. He needed help. The industry was accustomed to paying the band by feeding them some food, getting them all liquored up, providing drugs and a place to crash. That is the way it is done.

“Sure, I’ll help you,” I said. “I can negotiate contracts and deals and make sure they are paid properly. I’ll make sure you have gas money and can generate an income since this is your full-time job.”

And, most importantly, I wanted to see him successful in an industry that for “every 4 there will be 100,000 fallen”. Well, According to Vince Neil of Mötley Crüe. And a band that sold a million records worldwide might just have a clue on how to market.

Cali

After that, Tim kept asking me out.

I said, “No, I don’t date clients.”

This went on for over three months. He was persistent, I’ll give him that. He would text me, and on my flip phone, it would take forever to text him back.

This was way before you can send pictures, so he would email me pics of him and the band. He was cute, tattooed, and pierced. He’s a drummer, like Tommy Lee.

But he was a music company client and I don't date clients, personal rule.

After months of me saying no, his band fired us, dissolved the contract, and Tim wasted no time asking me out.

I said, “Give me a few reasons why we should go out.”

“Number one, we both like to text.”

“You gotta do better than that.”

“We both like music,” he says.

"Okay...You gotta do better than that."

"We both like to wear eyeliner."

Now, I've always been in love with Tommy Lee and Mötley Crüe. I'm assessing the situation, *"He's a drummer and he wears eyeliner. Instead of Tommy Lee, he's Timmy Lane. All right. Maybe."*

Then I said, "Give me another one."

"We both love me."

And I said, "Purely based on your narcissistic, self-absorbed, asshole attitude, you get one date."

"That's all you'll need. You'll marry me."

"You're full of shit," I retorted.

I accepted the challenge. He has balls and I like ballsy guys.

For our date, I picked him up at the train station in Newark, New Jersey and he's wearing green Chuck Taylor's, camos, a grey CBGB shirt, and an orange bandanna. I'm thinking to myself, "What the hell am I getting myself into?"

Then he hops into my Jeep and spills Gatorade and vodka all over the inside of my Wrangler.

That was the start of our relationship.

Tim

I had started wanting somebody I could build a life together with, to build a life with someone who could offer something, and we could be a team. A partnership was key. I always picked destructive people, and that's my destructive personality.

I went to prison twice because of the things I did, to get my money, in my addiction.

The first time I was in prison, all I cared about was getting out because I was a lot younger and all I was interested in was getting back to partying.

The second time I went to prison I knew when I got out that I wanted to be with someone who was productive, as compared to me being destructive.

I got out and spent a year getting myself together in my hometown of Titusville because I didn't have any money or anything. Then when I got a music opportunity in New York I took it.

Cali always makes fun of northeastern guys, but I've always wanted a northeastern girl. They're hustlers. They're business-minded. They don't want to just lay around and make babies. They want to do something with their life.

I knew I was going to find a girl up in the northeast. But I didn't date for the entire first year in New York because I wanted to make sure I knew what I wanted, someone who had dreams like mine. Someone that was goal oriented and had a zest for life.

I wanted someone who could offer me the lifestyle I could offer them. I wanted somebody who believed in me. I wanted someone who wanted to lock into a lifestyle together.

After I found Cali's company online, my band and I met her at Starbucks on 35th in Manhattan and as soon as I walked in, I thought, "Wow, this girl is gorgeous."

She's physically attractive, but it was more. It was her whole presence. She commands your attention.

If you're in the room with her, you're going to give her your attention, whether you like it or not, and that was really appealing to me. And that goes right with what I desired, to be with someone who knew what they wanted and what they wanted out of life.

Not to mention, the way she laid everything out in terms of how she was going to help the band, how we were going to do it, that appealed to me.

The four of us walked in, never knowing her, and she talked to us like she's known us her entire life. That was her personality. And that was extremely attractive.

We just fit.

And after we returned from Chicago I knew I was not going to quit asking her out until she said, “Yes.” I can be persistent when I want to be.

Cali

Tim was fun, no doubt. He knew how to have a blast on $10 in Manhattan which is an amazing skill. We would split a small bottle of gin and get a big diet coke and walk around the city. He made me laugh constantly.

We would eat the best falafel I ever had from the food cart for $5.00 he would say to me, "You don't need money to have fun, fun is free."

Fun, lots of smiles and laughter, all that was new to me and on the top of my "bucket list."

I had it, then lost it all, and I craved fun in my life, to travel and to be free.

I knew I wanted a guy who was tattooed and pierced. A guy who didn't own anything and didn't care about money. Someone who loved to travel and had a passion for life and was fun. Because I grew up in a house that had no fun.

Growing up, we didn't play and there was no vacation. We went nowhere and were always told there was no money to have fun. That was my requirement when it came to a guy. Must. Have. Fun.

Before we met, I had been single for two years. And most of the guys I met wanted a domesticated wife. Someone to cook, clean, and make babies. So, someone exactly not like me. I couldn't imagine a baby on one hip, spaghetti spoon in the other. No, that job was for my sister. She makes homemade pasta while I birth companies.

I'd sit down with potential suitors before we'd even talk. Tell them that I don't cook, I don't clean, and I don't do laundry. Most dates would end right there because I don't do those activities. I don't want to learn how to do them and I don't care about them, they're not important to me. Most guys left during the first 20 minutes of the date.

Tim sat down, and I told him the same thing.

"I don't cook. I don't clean. I don't do laundry. And I am not making any babies."

"Awesome. What do you do?" he asked.

I said, "I fuck, and I make money."

He choked a little and spit out his beer.

"Whoa, you gotta marry me."

Tim is the polar opposite of me, he loves to cook and to clean. He loves to do laundry.

He told me he wanted to travel around and play music and entertain people and make them happy.

I told him, “Sounds good, you do that, and I’ll handle all the financial stuff.”

Being in my mid 30’s and finding a guy who isn’t a 9 to 5 cubicle drone, with a stupid job, a house payment, obligations to a crazy ex and of course a ton of rugrats, THAT was the selling point for me.

I was the first girl that Tim brought around to his music scene friends who wasn’t a stripper. I didn’t have that overly sexual drive. I was the opposite of all these other girls. I was business oriented, I wanted to make money and travel and help people.

His friends didn’t know what to do with me because I wasn't wild and crazy, I didn't do drugs.

In the beginning, I was in still in Philly and he was in New York and he wanted me to see his apartment. He told me he lived in Times Square and I was impressed. A musician that can afford an NYC apartment, this was huge!

I went, and he opened the door to show me his place, a cracker-box, 10x12 room with three bay windows. Not an apartment, just a room. Amazingly enough, there was a sink and above it, there was a black magic marker arrow pointing down.

“Bathroom,” was the message. The microwave had a similar sign scrawled across it, “Kitchen.”

There was a community bathroom, a small, mildewed and dark closet down the hall.

Rent was $1000 a month for this little piece of paradise and I loved it.

It was cozy, it was quaint, and it was in Hell's Kitchen, just a few blocks from Central Park.

I remember the first time I stayed over in New York, I wanted to get up and go to the gym the next day. I always have had a hard time sitting still and when I told Tim he was coming with me, he cracked open a Natural Light beer.

Jokingly, I said, "If you want to date this, you have to go to the gym."

He took a plastic water bottle and filled it up with the beer.

"You're taking that to the gym?" I ask.

"Yup," Tim says. "You said 'go to the gym' you didn't specify 'no beer.'"

"Fuck," I say.

We go to the gym and of course, he's never trained, and he can't keep up with me because he's never worked out before. The beer is not helping either.

But, he is a natural athlete, and after I start training him a little, he gets results fast.

"I don't like that," Tim says. "I don't like this. That's too hard."

Then he tells me I'm training him wrong. He doesn't like being pushed, doesn't like the pain.

"Really?" I say. "That's wrong?"

But, in the end, he finally joined Gold's Gym with me and we began a partnership, me helping him stay fit and healthier than your average rocker. He would motivate me to get out of bed and moving before 10 am.

Tim

Once, when I went on tour and Cali stayed in my NYC apartment, she mentioned feeding the "cute little mouse" that came to visit. Little and mouse do not go in the same sentence in New York. I'm thinking "rat!"

Apparently, the "mouse" she was feeding animal crackers, went back and told his friends about Cali's buffet and when I got off tour they all came to visit.

One night we were sleeping, and I heard little sounds and one of them ran across my chest. It was cute until then. I plugged up the hole with spray foam, thinking that was the end of it. But, eventually, they chewed through it and came to eat again.

While I was teasing Cali about her new pets, she opened up to me about something that had been bugging her, about all of the "wild" women at the gigs I would play.

"I'm not like that," she said straight up.

"Number one, I don't share and number two, if you cheat on me, I'll leave you and that'll be the end of it," she assured me.

I didn't doubt her and told her I would never cheat on her.

"I want something stable."

I think we both realized at that moment, we were seeking something more adult, to settle down a bit, but still have the freedom to be ourselves.

Cali

I was still in Philly and Tim was in New York, but he would come over often, it was only an hour away on the train.

I was cooking dinner that evening and he called a little after 2:00 o'clock to tell me he'd be there at about 5:00 pm, but that he had to stop off beforehand, he was getting a gift for me.

At 5:00 o'clock he called again, informing me he was still in the city and couldn't find the gift.

"I'll be a little late, sorry."

When he still hadn't shown at 7:00 pm, I called him, "Hey, dinner's cold now, where the hell are you?"

"I'm still looking for your special gift, you're going to love it! I think I am heading to the right place now."

He strolled in at 10:00 o'clock finally, all dirty from his day, no bag in hand. I thought it must be jewelry in his pocket or something, I was super intrigued and anxious to find out what the "special gift" was that had kept him in the city so long.

"It's a 'private gift,' we have to go upstairs and then I'll show you," he says.

Of course, I'm almost going crazy with excitement, we hadn't been dating that long and he was buying me a "special, private gift!"

We get upstairs and he takes off his long-sleeved shirt, then his t-shirt.

He's got both nipples pierced. That's the "gift."

Tim slept on the sofa that night.

Cali

When we moved to Tampa, I was just rebounding financially. Musicians never have any money, and my music business was struggling. Tim was not touring much anymore so every penny we made went right to bills.

I was getting tired of the cold, and the glitz of NYC was starting wear thin. Tim was from Florida and I convinced him to return and show me around. I've always loved warm, sunny places.

When we first got to Florida, Tim and I had a small, one-bedroom apartment we could barely afford. We had a payment plan on the furniture and had a good laugh about that when Tim told me his furniture dealing stories. We struggled and at the same time, we got along great. We did really, really, well with no money.

Tim asked me to marry him with a $5 bottle of Barefoot wine and no ring. No fancy jewelry, just us on the beach and some weird fire twirler, practicing his performance behind us. We were on Clearwater beach and we crashed a wedding right after he asked me to celebrate.

Our wedding was a total budget wedding on the beach here in Florida. We had moved over to the East Coast by then.

We entered a contest and won a free wedding venue, but it was too far away from the beach. So instead, we rented this little building, for a couple hundred dollars. Tim's mom made all the food and we bought the cake at the grocery store. My dress was just a small white sundress. I didn't get my hair and nails done like the other girls, I really didn't care that much about it.

I had been taking Tim to all these Bridal Expos and it was at one of the expos where we entered the contest for the venue.

We always went dressed "rock n' roll" and Tim dresses sharp, attracting all kinds of attention when we go out.

A local photographer came up to me and said, "Your husband looks like Brett Michaels and my daughter loves Brett Michaels."

"Every year I give one photography package away for free to a deserving couple," she went on.

I was touched because we couldn't afford anything, and I told her our story.

The photographer, Tina Ortiz, and her husband ended up shooting our entire wedding and our engagement photos for free. A gift for which I am forever grateful.

Since we didn't have any money for decorations either, my sister and her fabulously domesticated skills saved the day. She dragged me to the Dollar Store and Walmart and we decorated the entire place for less than $100. And it was beautiful.

My Dad, ever the apple cart tipper, had a tantrum.

"I'm not coming to a redneck wedding. You're Italian and should marry Italian," he moaned.

I said, "Fuck you, then don't come. Make up your mind."

He and his latest girl-of-the-month ended up flying in the day before the wedding.

We didn't have any liquor, just a few bottles of wine and beer, barely enough for the guests. We couldn't afford a DJ so we took Tim's amp and blasted iTunes music through it.

We didn't do any toast and we didn't do any "couples dance." It was just two people getting married on the beach and it was awesome.

Nothing we do is traditional and we're fine with not fitting into conventional mainstream society. I think for both of us, one of our biggest fears, is being "normal," whatever that is.

We are perfectly happy being us. In many ways, I feel it's completely liberating to be comfortable within yourself.

Normal is just a setting on the dryer anyway.

Tim

The switch from cocaine to opiates was such a simple thing.

I was trying to find a coke connection and this one guy asked if I'd ever tried Roxys. He said they were pain pills.

So, I tried them. I just took them like a pill and I felt pretty good.

A couple of days later I got some more, and I swallowed them in front of the guy.

He asked me, "What are you doing, man?"

"What do you mean?"

"Dude, you should crush those suckers up and snort them, that's the shit," he says.

So, I did. And as soon as I snorted them for the first time I got it, I understood. It was the shit.

That's how the whole opiate thing started. It's also when I stopped using cocaine. It was a complete reversal. Usually, cocaine addicts are repulsed by opiates and vice versa. It was just a totally smooth transition for me, easy-peasy.

And the switch from Roxys and Oxys to heroin was because, at the time, Broward County really cleaned house with the pill mills. I couldn't find the drug anymore and that's when I got introduced to heroin.

A friend asked me, "Why are you getting sick when you can just go down to Liberty City and get heroin?"

I got a number, met a guy, bought six bags, snorted the first two and I was off.

The sickness went away, I felt great and it was cheaper than Roxys.

It was easy enough to start off with one or two bags of heroin a day to get high. It wasn't long before it got up to four bags a day, and it continued to escalate. It eventually peaked at twelve bags a day. $120 a day to basically stay high and mostly to avoid getting sick.

We were really scraping the barrel financially at the time and I started looking for alternative ways to get money. And that's when Cali started noticing that things were disappearing. I knew I was going to hit the brick wall, I couldn't keep up that type of spending.

First Date - NYC

Just Moved to Miami, Florida

Newly Engaged in Tampa, Florida

Engagement Photo Shoot

Engagement & Wedding
Photos Courtesy of
Ortiz-Sellers Photography

The Deadlyz, 2008

With Nikki Sixx of Mötley Crüe

Leggz and Tim

On the Stage with Vance Johnson

On CNN as Addictions Expert

Working Out....

...Working

Alaska Adventure

PART III

LIVING THE NIGHTMARE

"Drugs take you to hell disguised as heaven."
~ Donald Lyn Frost

Tim

I was able to hide my heroin from Cali because I wasn't a shooter, I snorted. And as a snorter, you're going to get a little bit of the nods, but nowhere near if you would if you'd stick it in your arm.

So, not being a shooter, and because Cali and I spent a lot of time apart, I was able to hide it for a lot longer. We didn't have a typical marriage where we'd both go to work 9-5 and eat dinner together and all that.

She'd be out in LA for two weeks and I'd be on the road for six weeks. She'd be in NJ, PA, LA, Vegas Colorado, Florida, New York, all over the place. And then that's when the usage would escalate.

When she wasn't around, I was bored and I could do what I wanted to and off I went.

Cali

I was in Vegas six months into his use and I called to see what he was up to, it was ten o'clock in the morning. I had gone back into private practice with clients and was building my addiction company back up from ground zero. This required a lot of hours and a lot more traveling.

"Hey babe, what's going on?"

"Numbthin' much...juss hangin'."

He sounded drunk. He doesn't drink at ten o'clock in the morning, and I thought to myself, "What's going on?"

And then he hung up on me.

He had never hung up on me before.

I talked to him that night and he seemed fine. But even then, my mind never went to opiates because he had always been an uppers guy. Most people who use cocaine don't do heroin. I couldn't figure out what it was.

He didn't mess with pain pills or morphine. He wasn't a heroin addict.

I was racking my brain, trying to figure it out.

What could it be? Maybe he really *was* drunk at ten o'clock in the morning. But that's odd, completely out of character. He'll go out and drink two or three beers but he's not a hard-core drinker. He won't close the bar, he gets bored. He's basically got A.D.D. and after two or three beers he wants to go home or walk on the beach or do something.

If he drinking at all, he likes to be social, not sit at home and drink alone, so why did he sound drunk at 10 am?

He hates benzos too, so it was not a Xanax nod or a Klonopin issue.

I couldn't put my finger on it and thought that maybe he was having some sort of stroke or seizures or something that was going to kill him.

I was seriously worried and when I got home from Vegas I started asking him questions.

"Tim, what's going on? Do you feel okay? Dizzy, lightheaded? Or anything? Because you sounded wasted the other morning...maybe you had a mini-stroke or something," I said.

His response was, "You don't know what you're talking about. It's not happening and you're just imagining it. I feel fine, I was just tired or something."

Tim

My drug habit eventually grew to 8-10 bags a day.

Miami went through a dry period, like any major city does, where the drugs are hard to come by and so the existing supply gets cut, blended, and weak.

I knew I guy who had a connection in Ft. Lauderdale, but the bags were $20, instead of $10, which I thought was weird, but they were a little bit bigger.

I started doing that for a couple of days and I noticed it was a little bit stronger. Or I should say, at that time, I thought it was stronger. I didn't realize it was just mixed with Fentanyl, to make you nod harder, to make you think it's stronger.

It was hard for me to leave the house on weekends because Cali and I would spend a lot of time together, so I couldn't hide it.

I bought six $20 bags to bring home with me on Friday night. I'd do a couple of bags late at night, while she was sleeping. I'd stay up and mess around on the computer or whatever. But, if she was asleep, I knew I could get high and not worry about her catching me.

I woke up at 7 in the morning, Cali's still asleep as usual and I still had two bags left. Mind you, I'm used to doing two $10 bags at a time, so I wasn't really thinking much of it. But I ended up dumping both bags out and snorting them.

I nodded out in the bathroom but then came to after a bit and ended up going to the couch.

My favorite thing to do was to have a cup of coffee after I'd do a couple of bags of heroin and watch Sportscenter. She'd get up to pee in the morning but then she'd go back to bed, and I'd be safe to enjoy my high for a couple more hours.

That morning I started feeling really, really, tired, so I laid down.

The next thing I remember was Cali kicking me in the chest. Ooof! The impact knocked the wind out of me and threw me way down into the couch. I shook my head, came to and she's standing over me with a phone in her hand.

"Did you just fucking kick me? What the fuck are you doing?" I'm yelling.

She had 911 on the phone and I could hear the lady asking Cali if she wanted to send an ambulance. I don't remember much but apparently, my lips were blue and a stiff kick to the solar plexus kicked my adrenaline into high gear.

Cali

Here's the unique part: I didn't mind the cocaine and the alcohol. It was never excessive, and he has such severe A.D.D., that when he does cocaine, you can have a conversation with him. When he's not on it, he's all over the place. He forgets his keys and forgets his wallet. He left his phone on the top of the car once and drove to the grocery store with it still on there.

We laugh this stuff off all the time, "Another Tim Moment!"

I know I will get slammed for saying it, but to me, Adderall is nothing more than synthetic legal cocaine.

That's why everyone is on it. The whole 'get him medicated' concept is simply ridiculous. Why put someone on a fake synthetic product that destroys their body? Cocaine is illegal and we, therefore, deem it bad but Adderall is legal, and doctor-prescribed, therefore it is 'good'. I can't wrap my head around that one.

I am totally into harm reduction, that's my specialty. Alcohol and cocaine don't bother me. Many of my clients are cocaine addicts that lead full lives using harm reduction. I also have clients that practice total abstinence. It depends on the drug and the person. I don't judge, I just assist them on their level and meet them right where they are.

However, there's no harm reduction with opiates.

If your drug of choice is alcohol, and it's unmanageable, then the best approach is abstinence. If your drug of choice is heroin, and you go out and have one glass of wine, then it's not a problem. If you have twenty glasses of wine, then we need to talk about that.

Cocaine and Marijuana are not often debilitating. They don't generally ruin your bank account. You don't disappear. You don't nod out and it does not become a manic obsession or a full-time job. Now for a few, this does not apply because it has destroyed their life, but I meet each person where they are and most of my clients fall into the former category.

I had no idea that Tim was using opiates for the first six months.

I think he started with Roxy and Oxy (synthetic heroin).

It was one or two here and there. He was still going out, doing stuff, and was functioning normally. It was when that six-month mark hit that I really started to notice something odd was going on and recognize behavior changes which pinged my "addiction radar."

There are two types of addicts. There's the addicts that can manage (functional addict) and the addicts that can't manage and then everything goes to shit. Usually, those who think they can manage eventually end up sliding on over to the other group.

Tim's that type.

He managed, managed, managed, and then it was, "Uh-oh. I'm stuck."

It's violent coming off the stuff. It's throwing up, diarrhea, terrible flu-like symptoms.

The first time he was coming off it, I totally thought it was the flu. The second time it was "food poisoning." The third time I knew something wasn't right, now I'm catching on that there's something out of whack here.

Nothing was out of place until he wasn't functioning, and these mystery illnesses were a huge red flag.

The weird thing is, in my twenty-one years of working in the addiction industry, I've never seen anyone go from using cocaine at sixteen, all the way up until they're forty and then switch to opiates.

When Tim was growing up, in an upper-middle-class neighborhood, cocaine was normal for those types of people. I'm from the 'hood and people from the 'hood use opiates to numb, usually because of trauma or depression.

When he switched to heroin, that threw me for a loop. There was no reason for him to touch that drug. No underlying root cause I could imagine. There was no trauma, nothing to numb himself to avoid or escape, life was great. We were traveling and enjoying ourselves, happy with our move to Florida and our new, fresh start. I had gotten back into private practice helping people with addictions and we were flourishing in Miami.

Tim

About sixteen hours after your last dose of opiates, you start to feel like you're coming down with the flu.

By the twenty-four-hour mark, it's like you have the worst case of the flu you've ever had. And by your forty-eight-hour mark, you're incapacitated. You can't get out of bed. You're vomiting, and you have diarrhea. It's like your case of flu has now been multiplied by ten and it lasts for three days.

You start feeling like it's never going to end and that's what usually causes people to go back. You start to feel insane, obsessing over the relief and high you would get.

By day four, you start coming out of it but you're still weak and you're still dehydrated, but you start to rebuild your strength.

Usually, I could bounce back in thirty days or so, but it got harder and harder.

That voice creeps into your head, the one telling you, "Just head on down to Liberty City with $40 and get high. Then everything will be corrected, and you'll feel great, man."

But it's a false correction, the drugs are just a temporary replacement for what your body can produce naturally if you can wait on it.

The waiting is near impossible, the voice is convincing and relentless. I've fallen prey to it a million times it seems.

Cali

The difference between cocaine and heroin is that cocaine has a 72-hour shelf life, meaning it wears off and there's not much for physical withdrawals, just cravings.

Heroin and opiates, on the other hand, have residual effects. Restless Leg Syndrome, insomnia, sweating, nausea, and vomiting. It's being easily irritated and exhibiting a flat affect.

You're into a detox phase quickly when you don't have your drug, but you have all these other problems when you're not able to get your drug, and it's obvious to anyone who's around you.

When you're on opiates, and detoxing, your body doesn't like what's in there, so every organ and every pore is trying to get rid of it as fast as possible. That's why you're sweating. That's why you're sick.

The person in withdrawal can't make decisions. I call it "talking to a wet napkin." They don't seem to have any personality at all, just flat, no emotion. It almost like they are just not there inside.

The brain has neurotransmitters that fire extremely rapidly when you do cocaine; bing, bing, bing-bing-bing. When you eat sugar, it's even more rapid than cocaine.

Cocaine is a bad drug, we can all agree on that, but sugar is probably worse. However, it's socially acceptable, so as a culture, we allow it.

Some people even encourage addicts to take sugar coming off opiates or alcohol, to get the dopamine back into your brain. So now they're sugar junkies. Amino acids work much better.

When you do opiates, the neurotransmitters misfire.

One will fire and the one on the receiving end, the one that's supposed to catch the signal, won't open. Then that one will open, fire, and the original one will close. Then they both shut down. And then the opiate hijacks your brain so now nothing works. It shuts down your neurotransmitters all together and the drug takes over your brain.

Opiates also ignite your pleasure center, which is what almost everyone is seeking. Pleasure, happiness, smiles, and laughter.

It's like having an orgasm, or eating a cheeseburger, or eating an ice cream cone. Your body thinks all this amazing stuff is happening, and then, when you take that drug away, your body doesn't know what to do with itself.

It takes a good week for your neurotransmitters to start firing again.

That's why people detoxing from opiates say, "I feel tired. I feel flat. I can't think."

As a spouse it heartbreaking and irritating all the same time. The person you are supposed to count on to help you and back you up is simply just not there.

Waiting for them to come back is even harder.

As a culture, we treat opiate addiction with more opiates like Suboxone and Methadone. This is basically giving a heroin addict more synthetic heroin.

Makes sense, right? Not really, because it's even harder to kick that habit once you get on it. I am all for using Subs to detox, but this idea to keep people on this stuff for years so they 'don't use opiates', makes zero sense. Suboxone IS an opiate. Once again, legal drugs are OK, illegal drugs are BAD. My brain just can't get it.

Cocaine and heroin in their purest form are natural. We try to get addicts off a natural drug and hook them on a worse drug and call it "maintenance in sobriety".

Your body then becomes used to using a synthetic, but it doesn't know how to go back to being normal.

But because street drugs are cut by drug dealers, and all this nonsense is added to it, it's nothing but chemicals now, no longer natural. It takes longer for detox and recovery.

It's also why heroin addicts have a hard time recovering. It's a physical drug, not just psychological like cocaine or speed. Heroin changes the body's chemistry and it is harder to function after getting sober.

People go back to using because their bodies don't want to reproduce the naturally occurring chemicals which have been replaced by the drug, it takes a long time for this to happen, and they get tired of waiting.

Think of it this way: you ride your bike up a long, steep hill. It takes 10 miles to get to the top. What point do you get off and walk the bike? It's hard, it's exhausting, and you are out of breath. Now imagine you have an electric bike that zips you right up that hill with zero effort on your part. How often would you use the electric bike? Probably every day. That's how opiates hijack the brain. The brain stops producing the feel-good chemicals because the chemicals you are taking are more amazing than its own juices.

Cali

As soon as I had an inkling about the heroin use, Tim got cut off from all our finances. He couldn't use our credit cards and he had no access to anything. Then I took his musical equipment, put it in storage, locked it all up, and took the key.

I had started taking my own advice. As a counselor, I would tell my clients, "This is what you do."

So now he's got no music equipment to sell. He's got no access to money and I took his car keys and hid them. I put them in my car, in my glove box, locked it up, and put my key on me. It's exactly what I tell my clients to do.

So now if he was using opiates, he'd be forced to detox, it was going to happen.

If he wasn't on opiates, well, I screwed up and I would apologize.

He started throwing up and that's when I knew the detox process had begun.

"You're going to lie on the bed. You're going to throw up and lay in your feces until you get a chance to clean it up. I want you to remember this experience," I told Tim.

He hated that and called me all kinds of mean, nasty names.

Remember, my father was a motherfucker and had called me all kinds of nasty names growing up. Plus, with almost 20 years in the addiction industry, I had heard it all.

"Call me anything you want, it's not going to phase me."

He wasn't ready for that response.

I knew with opiates you can detox cold turkey, or with the help of more opiates like Suboxone or Methadone.

Eventually, I started learning you can use CBD oil and Marijuana to lessen the symptoms of the detox.

Cold Turkey was my first choice with Tim, but it didn't work.

Tim

Where there's a will there's a way, right?

After Cali had me on financial lockdown and had I detoxed I was at Lowe's or Home Depot and found a receipt for some paint lying in the parking lot.

It reminded of a little scam I would run when I was younger, one I originally stumbled upon in my hometown of Titusville, so I thought I'd try it out.

The first time I had tried this it was a gallon of paint and I was walking somewhere and found a receipt for $49.99.

I went to the store and walked out with the paint, thinking I had a receipt to show for it. I waited awhile, then went back in and returned it.

I remember thinking later that was risky, walking out with the stuff, so after that, I would just never leave the store.

So here I am in the middle of the parking lot, receipt in hand and I think, "What the hell, might as well try!"

I walk in and go "shopping" for the item on the receipt, a couple gallons of paint. I find them easily and grab the handles, carrying them back and around the aisle, straight to the customer service desk.

"Hey, I got these, and my wife doesn't like the color or something, so she went somewhere else and picked out the paint she wants," I explained.

"Can I just return these? I didn't open them or anything..."

They were kind enough to give me cash back and off I headed to Liberty City, that little voice inside my head wouldn't quit and now I had free drugs.

I kept up the receipt scam for months, refining it so I could use my phone to know exactly where I would find the item on the receipt in the store. The SKU number would tell me what aisle, what bay, everything so I knew I had the exact item on the receipt.

Sometimes I was even scamming Cali. I would tell her I needed something, like a drill or whatever, maybe some cymbals for my drum set.

The truth was I had found a receipt for that item, but I knew they wouldn't give me cash back unless I could prove it was my card.

I would buy it with Cali's card, swap receipts and then return the item for the cash. She got a receipt which would "match" the statement and if I waited enough time to return the item, she wouldn't know it was missing and forget about it.

I was able to hide my use from Cali for a long time, especially since it appeared that I had money and was able to keep my use in check.

But eventually, I was running out of scams, receipts, and it doesn't take long to slip into detox.

There's a little bit of time before you know you're going to get sick where you know you can score and keep the ride rolling.

The next phase is when there's nowhere to get the drugs, you're out of money, and you are going to get sick. There is just no avoiding it.

Once I knew I was going to get sick, I knew it was time to fess up, time to admit it, to tell Cali I was using again.

We have property out in Colorado, so we went out there to detox, the theory being that I would have no access to heroin, no hookups.

It works the first two times we tried that plan.

The third time, I took forty bags of heroin with me.

I knew we were going to be out there for two weeks, so I thought that would be plenty. I ran through all forty in six days. And day seven dawns with that feeling of inevitability, the sickness is coming.

I'm out in the Rocky Mountains with no way to get heroin and I'm starting to get anxious and panicky. Cali had thought I was just detoxing because I had no energy and was tired. She didn't know I was high and that was going to become apparent in a few hours.

Cali

Heroin is a full body high, so it has a stronger hold on you than any other drugs. It is not just mental, it is physical, and it takes so long for the body to bounce back to normal that several attempts at detox and sobriety are common.

It's the worst withdrawal and worst detox from any drug I've ever seen. Your body needs heroin when you're detoxing from it. Your molecular structure changes and you need it. Your body now craves that drug. Heroin addicts crave heroin because their body has changed its chemistry.

It is like having that electric bicycle, you do not have to work, just zip up the hill.

That's heroin.

Your body says, "Do I have to pedal? I don't want to pedal!"

Then your mind tells you, "Dude, let's go to Liberty City with $40 and we won't have to pedal. Takes you ten minutes to get there. $40 is all you'll need."

That is why it takes so many attempts for a heroin user to get to recovery. Their mind is working overtime to convince them to take the easy way, to avoid pedaling.

Keep in mind sober is not recovered. That takes another 3 to 9 months each time you detox for your body to recover. And up to two years for your brain to really heal.

And an addict's mind will find all kinds of ways to justify the use and rationalize illegal scams, stealing from your grandmother or your kids, it is powerful.

It is crazy to watch and crazy to be on the team that helps the person get to recovery.

And while his brain was working overtime convincing him Liberty City was where it was at, I was working overtime trying to keep him in recovery, or so I thought.

With heroin, you can detox off heroin with smaller doses of heroin. It's not like cocaine. Had he given me the forty bags when we went to Colorado that time, I would've detoxed him myself. But he didn't do that and Tim being Tim, he took six or seven a day and it was gone in less than a week.

When it was gone, I locked him in the bedroom and went to the gym.

"You're going to throw up for the next three days. Bye!"

The only chance, at his age, of dying from detoxing off heroin, was dehydration. I bought Pedialyte, water, and Gatorade. That's all he got from me.

I offered, "Do you want to go to detox and rehab?"

"No," he said.

Residential treatment doesn't work usually, we know this.

Emotionally, he knows what he needs to do. But physically, the drug has him by the balls.

No treatment center can fix that with group therapy and the weekly "therapy session."

How do I know? I worked in plenty of them and the counselors are overworked and stressed out.

Half the time the staff can't even remember the client's name. There are simply too many clients per staff member and the expectation and pressure of getting them sober are huge. Add in the event of the stressful scenario of a client wanting to leave AMA (Against Medical Advice), you drop what you're doing and try to get them to stay. It is a crazy and chaotic mix.

When I worked in the treatment center world, we were told to stick the clients in "group." I am not a group therapy fan, I mean who is going to tell their deepest darkest secrets in a room full of strangers and expect a good result?

Plus, they sit and complain and hatch ways to get high and discuss new drugs.

One treatment center where I worked as a program director in Florida had a 50% fail rate every 45 days. That means that the same people kept coming through the program over and over. Our motto was "the addict must be not ready." I think the program is flawed. How can you have one hour of therapy a week and expect it to work? Even some of the new programs offer two hours a week. How does that really help?

It makes me think of trying to herd cats.

Now, don't get me wrong, I work with some amazing treatment centers. They have strong, effective clinical programs. They are clean, friendly, and can help someone find the path they need to recover. I personally tour every facility I recommend for my clients and meet the owners and staff.

The centers I don't work closely with tend to pump out mind-altering big pharma drugs to get the clients to remain calm and compliant. The therapists are exhausted and overwhelmed with constant paperwork.

And all this ineffective care comes with a hefty price tag, up to $70,000 with the schedules and time allowed for treatment dictated by the insurance providers in most cases.

No thanks, I have the skills and tools to help him myself.

We all do it. Everyone in this industry helps their own. We know what places to avoid, what places just 'put heads in beds', where the money game is, and we avoid them. With people going to treatment over and over and over and saying the 'addict isn't ready,' that infuriates me. That means the center does not have the proper tools to help the addict. Times have changed, treatment centers need to step up their game.

Colleagues help each other and their families too. We can all call each other at 3 am and offer assistance. It is what we do, we built our entire practice in crisis and helping others. We don't pawn off family members, we dive in and help each other.

No one says "Mmm, can I help my own friend or sister or father because someone says I shouldn't?'

No, we don't do that.

We help. We jump in and we help. We grab other professionals and we help.

I have assisted colleagues in the addiction industry and one was a treatment center owner who wanted to get sober again. One was a bigtime interventionist that advertises 10 years sober. Except he relapsed and didn't want to go into treatment.

It's simply what we do. We work at all hours and we help each other. No one says 'nope, I am not allowed to that because of some oddball unwritten rule'.

We save lives.

Sometimes it's unconventional. Sometimes it is controversial. But it works. And I am in the business of making things work to get people sober and into recovery. I don't ask questions. I just handle it. So, I did, I made calls to some of the best colleagues in the business.

Cali

Tim and I talked a lot for the rest of that trip. We strategized, we needed to figure out how to get him off opiates.

But regardless, the trust was gone, and I felt our marriage was crumbling.

When we returned to Florida, I called his brothers and asked them to come down to help. They said they would but never showed up. I tried to drop him at his parents' house but that was an absolute cluster fuck. No one was going to help me from his side of the family. His mom and dad were too busy enabling his two brothers and too worn out to help me with what was happening.

I was on my own.

I offered therapists, sober companions, sober coaches. I have the best team in the world at my disposal.

He declined. This was going to be a long process.

I made a deal and I put it out into the universe.

I was asking for one of three things: I hope he gets arrested and sober in jail, or he gets on tour with a working band, or I'm getting divorce papers.

"Manifest it and it shall be." I am super into the Law of Attraction and I use it for everything, I even teach my clients how to use it, it works.

Within twenty-four hours, I get an email saying that a well-known musician and group was hiring a drummer. The weird thing was, is that I hadn't put emails out there just yet. No one knew I was looking for Tim to get hired.

It was a rock-n-roll blues band I liked, and I submitted his website to the email. He got a response and they wanted him to audition.

I sent him to L.A. but I said to him, "If you go on tour, you have to come off heroin. You'll nod out at the drum kit and they'll fire you."

And he knew that.

He got the gig and when I met the crew Tim's touring with, I knew right away that they would party. I watched one of them shoot six double gin and tonics in thirty minutes and it didn't faze him.

I said to Tim, "He's a coke addict."

Tim didn't think he was.

They go on tour and Tim calls me and says he isn't detoxing.

He cleaned up in three weeks and had no symptoms.

"I don't have headaches," he tells me. "I don't have sweats, nothing."

I asked him what he was taking, I knew it had to be something, and he says, "Cocaine."

That was the first time I realized cocaine may be able to reset the brain after using opiates. I start researching it and found out that if you were a narcotics user before an opiate user, you can reset your brain using narcotics.

I was excited.

I knew heroin hijacks the brain and the body. I knew how it interacted, but to learn that a narcotic can reset the system? This was new, this was good news. And as always in my world, it was highly controversial, but then again some of the best solutions were controversial.

Tim

With Cali's help, I caught the break of a lifetime with this blues artist. It would've been great money and I would still be going to this day, but a big chain of events happened. Their old drummer quit, which opened the job for me.

I had been in a lull musically and I was still using regularly. Cali knew about it and she wanted me to go on tour, to keep me occupied, to get me out of town for a while.

She was submitting my portfolio and my website to anyone who would take it, behind my back.

Cali has this "law of attraction" thing she does when she wants something. So, when I came home there were papers all over the house. She had written that I was to go back on tour with a band and even how much she wanted me to make.

Cali is intense like that. When she focuses her energy on something she creates it and I played along.

About 3 days later, I got an email.

Eric Sardinas, who is somewhat like a modern-day Stevie Ray Vaughan, answered Cali and liked my stuff so they wanted me to audition.

I flew to Los Angeles and got the job.

They told me to meet them in Atlanta in two weeks and that they play three hours a night. But because I was using, I knew I had to clean up because if I detoxed out on the road I could ruin it.

I didn't want to stress Cali out, so I ended up detoxing with Suboxone on my own. Then I went out on the tour and it was a great experience. We were playing festivals and clubs, from Atlanta to Iowa. But they never gave me any hint that they were talking to their old drummer again.

They told me to get my passport ready for the European tour and I knew this was going to be the chance of a lifetime.

Cali had to run all over the place to get the passport application prepared and sent out, so I could get it in time. I was excited, and I was clean for the first time in a long time. I was happy and feeling pumped, getting ready to go to Europe.

We played the last show in Illinois and as we parted ways at the hotel, something felt weird. I was supposed to drive to Miami and then meet them back in Chicago in a few days when we would all fly to Europe.

But in a very unconventional way, as I was driving back to Miami, they announced on their website that their old drummer was back in the saddle and they were leaving for Europe the next day.

I called them to ask what's going on and of course, I try to lobby for myself. I had just busted my ass learning their music and bailed them out, but they didn't want to hear it. They simply wanted their old drummer back.

Cali was upset about it. She started crying and I said, "Hey, I'm the one who just lost my job. Why are you crying?"

She knew what it meant. I needed constant stimulation and now with music back out of my life, I was probably not going to remain sober. All that hard work and hustle for nothing.

So now I'm back in Miami, clean, and I think I lasted 72 hours before I'm using again.

PART IV

STUCK IN A LUCID NIGHTMARE

"Everything I was afraid of when I was growing up,
I've become. I've taken on my nightmares,
like the devil and the end of the world,
and I've become those things."
~ Marilyn Manson

Tim

As if the heroin epidemic wasn't dangerous and deadly enough, it has now been linked to deaths and overdoses from low-quality heroin or other opioids that are now laced with the deadly drug Fentanyl.

Fentanyl is 100 times more potent than morphine, so this should explain why people are dropping like flies after taking this drug without knowing.

One of the most well-known overdoses of Fentanyl was in Minneapolis with Prince. Prince had been taking opioid pills for years and on that fateful day the legendary musician took a Fentanyl laced Xanax without knowing it and died in his elevator before anyone could find him and revive him.

Now, as a recovering heroin user, I can tell you that you will never see a Fentanyl overdose coming. You have very little warning and when you do it is too late. I know this from experience because it has happened to me twice.

Let's revisit one of my Fentanyl overdoses just to let you know just how serious this can be.

I had just dropped Cali off for an appointment in downtown Miami and was basically looking to kill some time until she was done.

A normal person might go to Bayside and shop, walk along the downtown riverfront or head over to South Beach for an hour or two, but not me.

My idea of killing time was to drive to Liberty City and score a few bags of heroin. It's something I had done a hundred times with no issues at all. So, in my twisted mind, I'm not betraying my wife or really doing anything wrong at all. I'm just killing time until she is ready to be picked up.

I went to my heroin dealer's house. It was a typical day and he was nowhere to be found.

I bump into another guy who was riding by on his bike, an old dealer. I follow him around the corner and get four bags.

Then I lay my bags out like I always do, and I noticed it's white. Heroin isn't usually this white. I thought about this briefly, then I snorted it up.

For some reason, I decided to go visit my friend Willie, aka "Leggz," at his house.

Leggz was a bit of a legend in this neighborhood. He got his handle from some Italian gangsters who said he reminded them of an old Al Capone crony with the nickname "Legs" who did time with Capone.

Leggz cut his teeth doing B&E's, heisting jewelry and selling it to pawn shops, specializing in diamonds and other gems. The pawn guys knew he always had the best, and Leggz left his real name behind during that time, forty or fifty years ago. I don't think there's anybody around anymore who even knows his real name.

Anyway, I remember walking to his door and that's the last thing I remember.

Here, Leggz recounts what happened after that...

Well, one day I was here at home and the doorbell rang.

So, I go to answer the doorbell and it was Tim. And it's the first time he, you know, rang the doorbell at my house.

So, I was like shocked, you know what I'm saying. And plus, he came to the house and I didn't know he was coming. You know, this the first time this happened.

I tell him I say, "Give me a minute. Let me go in and get my keys and I'll be right back." So, I go get my keys and I come back.

And Tim is not at the door.

He's done and got back in his vehicle and he's sitting up under the steering wheel, you know.

So, I goes out and I say something to Tim and it wasn't Tim. You know, it was like it wasn't Tim. He was like comatose, just looking at me and stuff like that.

So, I say, "Damn Tim! Where you been? What are you doing now?" And he just looked at me, you know what I'm sayin', right?

And I say, "God damn, you done went and you did something. And now you messed up!"

So, I say, "Damn, I can't, you know, let nothing happen to you, I got to help you as much as I can."

Because I know when it comes down to Tim, he's got a lot of fear for his wife. And the fear is out of respect. And then plus he don't want to be embarrassed either, you know, letting her know that he's been doing certain things.

I'm saying, "Man, man, talk to me!" But he can't talk. He won't talk.

"Why the hell did this shit here happen now?!" And then I say to myself, "Well it's best that it happened, and he came here, because if he goes somewhere else, they would they would they would abandon him, you know?

Everybody would get out from around him, you know what I'm saying. They could help the person, but if the worst happens, then the police want to pressure them. Or give them a charge, you know what I'm saying?

You know, you don't have to be involved with it. You could have been close by and the dude made it to your house or the girl made it to your house. You know what I'm saying?

So, I go and go to helping him, helping him, helping him, helping him.

And I would get to a point where he would get moving like slowly, slowly, but I see that I'm not doing, basically, enough, you know?

So, I said, "Man, God damn man, it's best for me...to call the paramedics."

And my mother is in the house, she's 91 years old, 91 years. So, you know, I didn't want to have to call, but it's a life involved. You know what I'm saying?

And I just go to help, and I call the paramedics. The paramedics come and it's like three of four men in the vehicle and it was lucky that it was, you know. Because you have to move dead weight, you know, a body. One person, maybe you can move them if is not under those circumstances, but the fact is that under those circumstances, you're not capable of moving them.

So, and he's up under the steering wheel. The paramedics get the seat adjusted where we were sliding him, and it took, like, three of them to get him up on the gurney. We put him on the gurney and they take him around to the back door of the paramedic's truck and they put him in the truck and they go to assist and kind of work on him.

So, they asked me, "What happened to him?"

And I'm not saying anything, you know, hoping that he'll come around, so he can tell him what took place, you know what I'm saying?

But, by me knowing him and the feeling that he has for his wife, I know he's not going to say a damn thing. He's not going to say nothing for embarrassment. Plus, you know you how a man can be in control of women, but in certain times, the woman is in control?

You understand what I'm saying? You know the woman is in control in this situation... it's out of embarrassment...

And plus, he knows that he's going to have to suffer, you know, the consequence of whatever is going to go on in the household afterwards.

And so, he's in the truck with the paramedics and they keep asking me, "Was there an accident? What happened? What's wrong with him?"

I say, "Man, I don't know, basically, what happened."

"But, by me knowing him and knowing what he likes to do, I think he went and got himself some H."

They say, "Well, we wanted to know, but basically we can see that by looking at his pupils." Paramedics and doctors do that, they can tell by his pupils that he's up under the influence and it's clear whether he is on an upper or downer.

"Maybe he done gone and got some bad H, you know what I'm saying?" I tell them, and they say, "Damn..."

But they want to hear it come out of his mouth.

So, they done hit him one time with a Narcan. And it brings him around a little but it's not enough and it's not effective enough. It's not enough. You know what I'm saying?

It does make him respond a little to it, but not come to completely.

They hit him again with the Narcan.

They keep asking him, "What you on? What you on?" And he is lying there, just lying there, you know, and they look at me and I say to Tim, "Man, tell the people what you on!"

He'd look at me and I know he's not going say anything.

When certain things happen, I get emotional, when I get emotional and my voice starts to raise. I just raised, you know, my voice and I say, "Fuck this! Tell the motherfucking people what the fuck you on, man!"

"It's time to motherfuckin' come clean, man! Fuck that shit with you and Cali right now...I got great respect for you and her," I tell him.

She knows me and feels a little more comfortable because she knows I'm not going to abandon Tim. And that I got a 45-year history. I got caught up when I was 15 or 16 years old on that and had been fucking with it ever since so I've had a 45-year history of it. And I told her about it, you know.

So, I'm there and I'm telling him, "Right, man, fuck this shit man, you got to tell them, you know what I'm saying?!"

"You just got deal with Cali later, goddammit if you don't tell these people what's going on and something

happened to your ass, then Cali's gonna come around here and kill my motherfuckin' ass, man!"

"You tell these people man, so they can save your life!"

The one guy says, "He's done, let's call it."

And I'm starting to get worried, and scared, and I'm telling them, "Try again, try again." Because I'm scared for Tim and Cali.

The other paramedic says, "One more."

The paramedics hit him again with another Narcan and he started coming around, slowly coming around, slowly coming around, slowly, and he came out of it.

And he came out of it jumping and waving.

The paramedic people say, "Damn, Tim if it wasn't for your associate here, man, you probably would have been dead, you understand me? Because you had flat-lined twice! Flat-lined... twice."

And they say, "Man, if it wasn't for this guy, you'd be dead."

He say, "Normally people in that position would get out from around here, that man had a lot of heart to assist you like that."

And so, Tim told them everything, and came around.

After going up to Leggz's door, the next thing I remember is someone screaming, "Tell them what you took motherfucker. Tell them what you took!" I couldn't see but I could remember that.

It was Leggz trying to save my ass.

I was finally able to open my eyes and realized I was in an ambulance.

I'm lying on a gurney and have all these cops or paramedics around me.

It's total confusion when you come out of an overdose, but once I regained my senses the first thing I thought of was how much time had passed during my OD and was my Cali okay and was she wondering where I was.

That is the first thought I had of her.

Suddenly, I coughed up the three plastic bags.

It's a weird thing I do. I chew on the bags after I snort them. I must've swallowed these ones.

As soon as I did that, the paramedics knew I was on an opiate, but they didn't know which one.

I kept denying it.

Then they tell me that they had given me three shots of Narcan.

Usually, it takes one time to do it. They almost never go over two. And I got three.

I finally admitted it was heroin.

I came to and refused medical treatment. I signed a sheet of paper, admitting as much, and then Leggz put me in my car and started driving me around.

The Narcan flushes everything out, so I wouldn't get sick and after an hour and a half, I feel fine.

I was dead a couple hours earlier and then I felt completely normal.

Leggz is telling me, “You know, man, you better go and straighten up and clean up everything that you can, go and deal with Cali.”

“You know you go you have to deal with this shit because you got paramedics here and they made a ruckus and they’ll be mail showing up at your house and you know you won’t be there to pick it up.”

I drop Leggz off and call my cocaine dealer because I was feeling a little groggy.

Luckily, I was able to pick Cali up on time. She never knew anything was wrong.

I was dead a few hours ago and she has no idea she’s married to a junkie.

I didn’t tell her anything right then, I decided to sit on it, think about it. It was all so surreal and weird.

As more and more time has passed since that day I think about just how close to death I was, and I can't imagine what I would have put the love of my life through if she had to bury me.

Tim

Six months later, I flatlined again.

I had come off a little tour and I was clean. I don't know what triggered this episode because when I got back to Miami, everything was going great. I hadn't been using at all for a little while, so my system was clean, I was past any withdrawals and feeling healthy.

I got five bags and did two or three, snorting them like I always did, and I remember driving out of the 'hood and I could feel this big wave, and I kind of knew I was in trouble.

Evidently, somebody had tailed me out of the neighborhood.

The thugs look for out of place people, people with expensive cars and I was driving our BMW which was like a big red flashing light in that neighborhood, and then they tail you. They get in front of you at a traffic light and step on their brakes, so you end up hitting them.

It was a scam.

I had already had a few incidents on my insurance, so he offered to call it a wash and not call the police if I paid him $50.

I followed him to the ATM, to this little bodega, and things were really starting to slow down for me at that point. My vision was getting blurry, but I didn't really think I was in that much trouble. I just thought I was really, really high.

And I was. I was so fucked up that I couldn't remember my PIN or any of that.

At that point, the guy behind the counter knew something was wrong and quickly, I felt really feeble. I looked at the clerk through heavy eyelids, tried to say something, and then I collapsed.

The owner of the store didn't want anything to do with me and took me out to the sidewalk and just let me lie down.

The next thing I know, I wake up in the back of an ambulance, I open my eyes and they ask, "What's your name?"

"Tim," I mumble.

"Where are you? What city are you in?"

I tell them with confidence, "Dallas."

Now, I'm in Miami, Florida, but the last city my band was in, was Dallas, and for some reason, I subconsciously thought I was still in Texas.

They asked me, “What did you take? What are you on, buddy?”

“I scored some really bad heroin from the last club we played at here in Dallas.”

The paramedic tells me, “Dude, you’re in Miami. We just loaded you up with Narcan, you were gone.”

I ask him, “Where’s my BMW?”

“What BMW?” he asks.

Then he tells me they must admit me to the E.R., but I’m not having it. Last time at Leggz’s they didn’t admit me but they’re not letting me go this time.

But they can’t keep me long. I sign myself out and I ask the woman at the desk, “Can you tell me where they picked me up?”

She gave me an attitude and didn’t want to tell me because she figures I’m just going to get high again.

I find the guy who brought me in and I ask him if he can tell me where I was before they brought me in and he tells me.

It was about ten blocks from the hospital, so I start walking and things start coming back to me.

I find the bodega and when the guy behind the counter sees me, he runs around the counter and hugs me and says, “I thought you had died!”

“I did, kind of. Did you call the paramedics? Thanks for that...”

He fills me in on what happened.

It turns out the guy who was scamming me also stole my BMW. But I don't think he knew there were five bags of heroin in the car.

I waited three hours to call Cali and I told her, "I got tapped by someone in the car. I went into the gas station to get a pen and paper and when I came out, the car was gone."

She didn't believe a word I said and knew instantly that I had been rolled.

When the hospital bill came for the second time, she had proof. Of course, I told her the guy who hit me used my information, but she knew the truth. She is one tough cookie.

Thankfully we had LoJack on the BMW and the cops found it.

In the car, they also found his gun, his knife, and my heroin. The guy they arrested got a dope and gun charge too, on top of grand theft auto.

I ended up telling them I couldn't ID the guy because I couldn't.

I had been too high.

Cali

Tim told me about his deaths a month later.

He's a great liar, but only when he's using, and he kept it from me because he wasn't sure how I would react.

He had been telling me things for some time, but my gut would tell me something else, wondering if he was using or not.

I would go searching for clues. I would search his pants pockets. I would search his truck. I would search his musical equipment, his toolbox. Everywhere. I was like a maniac, looking everywhere.

Why can't I find empty baggies? Why can't I find pillboxes? Why can't I find something?

I had always wanted to be an FBI agent, so my Private Investigator skills are on point.

Then I'd ask him to take a drug test and he'd tell me that that wasn't right, that I shouldn't ask my husband to take a drug test.

And he's right, I shouldn't. But that was just another big red flag.

At one point, I was even tracking his phone, to try and prove he was in Liberty City.

So, my gut's been telling me he's using drugs, but I have no proof.

Now I'm stuck, either waiting for him to tell me something or slip up or maybe, just maybe, he's right and my gut is wrong.

Then one day he tells me, "Hey babe, I gotta tell you something, I want immunity."

Immunity?

Most times, deep dark secrets are of the cheating kind, but he would never cheat. He's not that type.

He has crazy ex's that have multiple husbands with multiple kids and he hates that concept, I know it's not about infidelity.

I'm thinking, "I have heard it all, so what could he tell me that I don't know?"

"I died of a drug overdose. A couple times now."

Now, that I didn't know. That I wasn't expecting.

We were driving in the car when he told me. And the silence was immense for what felt like an eternity but was probably ten seconds or less.

"I need help, can you help me?" he asked.

He told me he can't do it, can't find a way to stay clean and that he doesn't know what to do.

"I kind of want to try Suboxone, the right way," he says.

The Suboxone is great for the acute symptomology but post-acute is a bitch. That is when they all go back out to score. The brain fog, the insomnia, the restlessness, the lethargy. You either end up on the Medically Assisted Therapy (MAT) for a long time or deal with the post-acute withdrawal.

I know how Tim felt about Suboxone and the doctors who prescribe it, he thinks they're pushing their drug, that they're a legal dope dealer.

I know he's got a buddy that started off a thirty-day detox with Suboxone, he's a musician friend. And he's now on about year nine of his Suboxone detox.

They just keep writing his script, and they keep filling it and he is going to be in for one hell of a detox when they decide that they don't want to write his script anymore. It could very well kill him. I mean, it really could.

All his teeth have fallen out.

He's mid-thirties and he jumped out of the back of a pickup truck, and his ankle snapped. One of the things Suboxone does with long-term use is it takes the calcium out of your bones, so they become extremely brittle.

I had a plan.

"Let's use it just for detox and let's try the CBD oil again," I suggest.

But as usual, the detox doctor overprescribed and wanted to put him on "The Suboxone Maintenance Program", at 32 mg a day, which is absolutely fucking ridiculous. Then up it to over 50 mg the following week.

Typical asshole doctor. I was very specific what I wanted on the protocol. I wanted him to come down and detox at 8 mg, then 2 mg.

The idea is to use it as a detox protocol, not an ongoing maintenance plan.

The definition of detox is "a process or period of time in which one abstains from or rids the body of toxic or unhealthy substances."

With the Suboxone, unless it is truly used as intended and not for maintenance, it's just giving the addict an unhealthy chemical to get them off a chemical.

That means the client is never really detoxed, the cycle is prolonged.

This "lets' get them off heroin and hooked on a big pharma opiate" is nuts. The eventual detox off that stuff is even worse than the organic heroin. It's longer and more painful.

Tim took the Suboxone for five days and weaned himself off.

The doctor called, "Where is Tim? He had an appointment every week."

This doctor, who was charging $350 for each appointment, was fully intending to increase the dosage.

I intercepted the call, "You're a legal drug pusher! I will not send a client to you to up dosages to get them hooked."

I was so sick of not having answers to solve the heroin addiction problem, not just Tim's, but other clients I was working with who had similar issues, relapses, and overdose experiences. The shit was getting out of hand.

I started reaching out to other professionals looking for answers.

Naturopaths and Chemists. Holistic healers, Chinese Herbalists, Medical Marijuana Doctors. I started talking to them all and networking.

"There has to be a better solution," I told them. "If there isn't one, let's create it."

But figuring out an effective solution was going to take time and I didn't have much time. Clients, friends, everyday people, and now even my husband were dying every day, all around me.

Tim

This time it wasn't a complete flatline, call the ambulance episode, but I had picked back up again, relapsed a little right in the middle of this clean-up.

I was doing some rehearsals, getting ready to tour with my band CrowFly and I had snuck some dope into rehearsal.

We were rehearsing, and I remember it like it was yesterday, I just remember almost feeling like I was going sideways, like my balance was going off.

The rest of the guys in the band later told me that we got about three or four measures into the second song of the set, they just looked at me and I was out.

I was completely nodded out, leaning against the back wall still on my drum throne and they just stopped and stared at me.

They knew what was going on right away, but they didn't know what the hell to do. My singer and my guitar player picked me up, Brandon and Dave, and they had to usher me out into my truck through the side entrance where the owner of the facility couldn't see what was going on.

The guy that runs the facility doesn't like drugs or alcohol or anything, he doesn't even let open containers of alcohol into his rehearsal studio. He doesn't want the headache of underage kids in bands drinking and then he gets sued, that story, so he runs a tight ship.

They put me in the back of my truck and started asking me, "Dude, what's wrong, what's wrong? Did you ... I mean, are you on heroin? What's the problem?"

I guess I told them, "Yeah, I am."

I was prepared for this, like heroin addicts who have overdosed often do, because I had the fear of going out. I was worried about having to get another Narcan revival, so I had cocaine on me too.

And I just told my singer, I said, "Brandon, there's a twenty-dollar bag of coke in my left front pocket, get it."

By this time, I was out of it and I said, "I don't care how you have to do it, get it in me!"

And it was almost like my own little Narcan, but it was cocaine and he just took the straw, dipped it into the bag and almost like siphoning gas out of a gas tank, they just put it right up my nose.

Almost instantly I just popped up, "Alright, let's go! Let's finish rehearsal."

They couldn't believe it, "No, you're gonna sit here and you're gonna give yourself forty-five minutes to get yourself together."

They went back in and started running the set without drums and they came back out about forty-five minutes later. I was like a little dog in a cage in the back of my truck, excited and ready to go.

"Alright, let's go finish rehearsal," they said quietly, shaking their heads.

We ran the set for another hour and it sounded phenomenal.

I've had some bumps in the road, small ones, and big ones. People think recovery is where you just decide you're going to get clean and you click your heels three times and six to eight weeks later you're completely clean with no hiccups.

But, shit happens.

Recovery is not instant and you're going to have mess ups and you have to just fight through it and if things like that happen it's not the end of the world. You must get up, brush your ass off, and keep fighting, it really is a life or death battle.

Cali

I knew something was up again. I was traveling, in Los Angeles for a TV show appearance, and when I called Tim one morning he sounded fucked up.

"Are you drunk?" I asked.

"No, I'm just tired. I'm just tired."

I've heard this line of crap before and when I tried calling back, he wouldn't answer his phone all day. What the hell is going on?

After I got back from that trip, he comes home from work and goes right to bed, telling me, "I'm exhausted."

"Exhausted from what?"

Red flags all around me and then the icing on the cake, no sex, ever.

Now, what am I going to do?

For some reason, I figured maybe a cross-country road trip would help.

Tim

Cali decides we need to go on a trip, to get out of Florida, to get me away from my triggers.

I stock up on a bunch of heroin and even get some methadone to take the edge off in case I run out before we get back.

The plan is to fly to Alaska, check it out, then fly down to Seattle where we would get in a car. We would take our time road-tripping and drive over to Montana, through Yellowstone and the Tetons, then on to Colorado.

I was back into full-blown addiction and managed to burn through my heroin while still in Alaska and started tapping into the methadone tablets.

Obviously, I did not bring enough and started detoxing while in Seattle. Cali loves Seattle and I had never been, so she was super excited to show me around. But all I wanted to do was lay around the hotel.

She's trying to get me to go out to eat, go for walks and stuff and I had no appetite, no energy.

We leave Seattle and start heading to Idaho on our way to Montana. We get to Coeur d'Alene and I was really feeling crappy.

Cali's all excited, "Let's check out the lake, let's grab a bite!"

I barely made it through lunch, didn't eat a thing and we went back to the hotel. I was lying down and in bed by 3 pm, "I don't feel so hot, kinda shitty, I need a nap."

The next thing I know, Cali's kicking me awake.

"You stupid ass motherfucker! You've got restless leg, you told me you were clean!"

I stammer some shit like, "I just... I took some Suboxone." And then promptly threw up.

"You didn't take Suboxone, that's bullshit," she says. "That's fine, I'm going to get some dinner and then go sit by the lake."

"And then tomorrow we're getting up and you're driving."

She made me do the driving after that and I was so sick, I'm puking in the car. Cali's unfazed.

"I hate you!" I tell her at one point.

"You can hate me all you want, you're driving and I'm enjoying the ride," she says.

I'm sick as a dog as we drive into Montana and spend the night. The next day we head to Jackson Hole, through the Tetons. Cali's ecstatic, she loves the scenery and makes me stop at all the little lakes and scenic overlooks and stuff.

It's cold as hell and I am now miserable, fully detoxing, my body unable to regulate temperature and she's making me get out and walk around the little lakes.

It's her birthday and she wants to celebrate by getting some sushi while we are in Jackson. If I could vomit any more, I would.

"You're not getting a Hall Pass from me," she says. "I don't care how you feel. I saved up for this trip and planned it and we're here. It is on my Bucket List, and I am going to see it all.

We finally make it to Colorado and I'm telling Cali I need some Methadone or Suboxone or something. She's having none of it, in fact, she's almost enjoying my misery.

I get on Google and do a search "how to score heroin in Denver" and no shit, there are some instructions.

I find these little forums where people are telling what street to go to, who to look for, how to motion to them. So off I went to the Cherry Creek bike path.

It was way too easy and soon I was walking back to my car with some black tar heroin. It's all they do out in Denver I guess.

I have never used a needle in my body, always snorted my dope, so now I'm back on Google figuring out how to snort black tar.

What a mess.

Cali

We drove to Denver, then flew home. Tim had finally worked through his detox. I didn't know about the tar then, but he later told me it was such a pain in the ass and he did not want to use a needle, he quit trying to score.

We tried marijuana to help with his detox and reduce his cravings. Very few people have a reaction to marijuana, and Tim's one of them. He ate an edible marijuana cookie and started tripping like he was on LSD. For three days.

One of the problems with heroin is once you finish the throwing up piece, you have anhedonia so bad you just want to use again to feel better emotionally.

Your brain is foggy you have no energy. You're irritable, depressed, and just have no joy in your life, no reason to smile even.

Tim would get five, six, seven days, ten days clean but he could not get past that hump.

The one time we made it 40 days and he would say, "I still feel like shit. Like, I was good for two days and then I feel like shit and then I feel good."

And then he would sweat out of nowhere. He's totally feeling fine, has tons of energy, thinking he's past it. Then out of nowhere, he'd be sweaty he'd have Restless Legs. He's all bitchy and no fun, and that's when he would always go back out use.

And when he would use just once or twice, he'd be right back in the cycle. So that's what kept him sucked in. No matter how far we got he never felt good enough to get past it.

We had to find a way to overcome the anhedonia, the inability to feel any sort of pleasure or happiness with life.

We were becoming pros at dealing with the detox, Tim was even self-medicating with Suboxone off the street, weaning himself from heroin on a regular basis.

But it wouldn't last.

Tim

"You're a bitch! A total cunt!"

Cali had shut off my access to the bank account, and whenever I needed money, I had to go to her and plead, tell her exactly what I needed it for.

And now she was harassing me about a charge at the hardware store, something that showed up on her account and I hadn't gotten her a receipt.

"What the fuck is this for?!" she demanded. "Bitch, cunt, really? That's the best you've got?"

I know her Dad was super verbally abusive when she was younger, and she wasn't going to be fazed by my name calling.

I took a picture of the receipt and texted it to her, told her, "I'll see you later, sorry I forgot to tell you about the charge."

I got home a little later and all my stuff was gone. All my musical instruments, anything of value was nowhere to be found.

I waited for hours, tried calling Cali repeatedly, but she didn't answer her phone or text messages. I thought maybe she was gone for good, I don't know, tired of my shit.

I was sound asleep, and she poked me awake.

"Where were you?!"

She said flatly, "Out."

"What were you doing?"

"Nothing," she replied.

I just looked at her and she says, "Now you know what it's like!"

"Don't ever do that again!" I yell.

"You do it all the time!"

I realized then you have no control, you have no idea where your spouse is, and this is the kind of shit addicts pull on their families all the time. Disappearing and then re-appearing with some dumbass story, totally unbelievable. Making promises they never keep.

Cali was teaching what it felt like to be on the other side of the coin, to be the loved one of the addict.

She had recently pulled another "learning moment" on me.

"I'm gonna buy Dallas Cowboy tickets for the home opener," she told me. The game is in September, this was in June.

All summer, "I'm buying these, we're going to get front row seats, you know, fifty-yard line."

A week before the game I'm getting pumped, "When's our flight?"

"Oh, you know, I haven't booked it yet, but I'll get to it. I'm going to get to it tonight."

And the next day, "When's our flight?"

"Oh, you know, I'm working on it, I'm going to get it done today."

And then it's almost game time and I'm freaking out, "When the fuck are we leaving?"

She says, "Oh, I spent the money on something else! You wanna see the new shoes I bought?"

"You gotta be fucking kidding!"

I was pissed, pissed!

"How does that feel?" she asked calmly.

"You tried to teach me a lesson using the Dallas Cowboys, that's not fair! You know I love the Dallas Cowboys, that's sneaky," I cried.

"You're going to learn, you're going to learn when I do it back to you, and that's the only way you're going to learn," Cali told me.

"Because I tried the nice love, I tried the tough love and that didn't work."

She went on, "I'm just going to mirror your behavior and you can get to see what it feels like, and when you feel that, that uncomfortable sadness, you're going to stop."

Cali

Tim is fantastic.

He's not narcissistic and he has a huge heart and an amazing personality. He's confident as fuck and I may be biased, but I think that's very attractive. He's superb in bed. He is a tattooed and pierced rock n' roller. He is everything on my list and I love him immensely.

His generosity is tremendous, I've watched him take his only dollar and hand it to a homeless person. He will order a cheeseburger and give it away and not have anything left for himself.

He is the kind of guy who can wear a badass outfit (not a suit) in a room full of CEO's or flip-flops and a tank top and hang out with the homeless guys in the street. But he doesn't own a suit. I love that.

People ask why I stayed with him through his heroin overdoses, his lying and sneaking around. Why didn't I just take off?

What kind of addictions coach would I be if I can't do what I'm telling my clients to do? What kind of wife just abandons her husband because he has a problem? He's my family. He's my husband for fuck's sake.

When I met him, he was not a heroin addict, had never done opiates.

Occasionally alcohol and cocaine with the band or whatever, sure, but not heroin.

Never.

When he started using opiates at almost 40 years old, it caught me off guard. I had been with him for a few years before we had gotten married and I had never seen signs of use and I didn't suspect anything for a while.

Why do people suggest "divorce him, dump him, abandon him" at his lowest point?"

Possibly because they're quitters or they don't want the headache. They get tired of the lies, the loss of money, the constant stress and worry.

Maybe they don't understand addiction like I do, it's a tough one to figure out and there's a lot of misinformation out there. Sure, you can toss them out, but you don't abandon them. Rock bottom is a fallacy.

Addiction is way more than just a disease, there is an attachment component to it and of course the reward deficiency syndrome. It is more than "hit bottom, go to treatment, go to meetings, surrender your will to God and pray."

Sure, that might work for a very small portion of those suffering from substance abuse.

But who just walks away? If he was my son, I wouldn't walk away. And what kind of professional would I be?

When he overdosed I did everything I tell my clients and I followed my clinical advice. I followed the protocol I had been suggesting to others.

Nothing worked. I even threatened divorce, but he kept using.

Maybe I had been enabling, a common challenge for spouses and families of addicts. The big question is, "Am I enabling or helping?"

I think the first time I enabled him to continue his drug use was when he had pawned a bunch of stuff and I helped him get it back. He had some bullshit story I believed, and once I realized what was going on I made a commitment to not do that anymore.

He would get himself into situations like the pawning deal and I would just tell him, "I'm not helping you."

And he would start in with the "Please, baby" and the "I love you" and the classic addict manipulation tactics. I would just walk away, go to the gym or something.

Then I started evaluating if I was codependent. Was I a co-dependent person that had to be with him? Some of my clients are, they simply stay because their self-worth is tied to their husband or wife, their identity even.

No, I didn't think I was co-dependent.

I have enough money and I can go wherever I want. I can work from anywhere, I'm totally mobile.

Then it became a challenge, I live for "challenge" and hate losing, I knew I had to make him stop.

I had to learn, and I had to figure out what was happening, somehow get to the root cause.

Somewhere along the line, something went wrong, and I was involved in that, I couldn't just walk away.

I did everything I could think of, including calling his family, and he wouldn't stop. They didn't do anything, they didn't visit...nothing. I thought maybe, just maybe, I would have them as an ally, backing me up, but no such luck.

When I asked them for help, they responded, "Help with what?"

"Well, Tim's detoxing again and he's been throwing up for three days, he's a heroin addict you know."

"Are you sure he doesn't have the flu? Do you think maybe you should take him to the E.R.?"

My family was equally useless.

"Divorce him," was the best advice and offer for help they could muster.

My Dad even went on a little rampage, "Oh, my daughter is married to a heroin addict, a red-necked heroin addict!"

He kind of lost his mind over the whole thing, and I had to tell him, "You know what? I'm done with you too if you're not going to be helpful!"

Most families bond together and help each other but not here. No one wanted to be bothered, no one wanted to hear it, I was left to deal with it alone.

I think a big part of me not giving up was because my father has been married four times. I didn't want to live that way, to have a revolving door for spouses.

Another part of it was, if I was sick, with cancer or something, would he leave me? There's going to be a point at some time where I'm going to need somebody. I sure didn't see my family flying down to help me anytime soon. Or his for that matter.

I so wanted to see him better himself and fix himself. I missed the man I met in New York City: the CBGB-shirt/Chuck Taylor-wearing, fun person I met and fell in love with.

Opiates took him from me and I'll be fucking damned if I gave up and let them win.

PART V

THE AWAKENING

"Only three things can change our lives: dreams, suffering, and love."
~ Paulo Coelho

Cali

Tim's last relapse was when his father died, and I knew it was coming.

His band CrowFly was playing their first show together after working out the kinks and rehearsing for months.

We were there at the venue and Tim walks in and he's pasty white.

I said, "What happened?"

He'd been clean, no drug use for four months, I was so proud of him.

And he says, "My brother just called, my father was just diagnosed with cancer."

They're ready to go on, it's five minutes from showtime, first show they've ever played together.

I called his brother and I lost it, "You stupid ass motherfucker, this is the first show CrowFly has ever played together and you call right before the show with that information?"

"You can't wait an hour until they're done and tell him?"

Tim was a wreck, a total mess.

As they're up there playing, the singer's girlfriend comes over to me and she's pasty white too.

"What happened?" I ask.

She says, "My mother was in a car accident. My mother was in a car accident in West Palm Beach, she's in the ICU."

She's freaking out.

CrowFly plays their set, Tim comes off and the singer's girlfriend comes over and they're all standing there.

She flips out, her mom is in the hospital.

Tim's also a little wigged and says, "We gotta go."

All his friends and the band member's friends were there, and they hadn't seen him in years, so this was a big deal. There's probably a hundred people in the club, but eighty of them were there for them.

Tim is still insisting, "We gotta go, we gotta go."

So, he packed his stuff up, and we went to the family, his Dad was in the hospital, went to see his dad. Brandon, CrowFly's singer, and his girlfriend left for West Palm Beach.

Tim's Dad had been diagnosed with terminal cancer. It was like the weirdest, strangest thing, he went from being totally healthy to dying, that fast.

We came back home, and I was like, "Oh, shit."

I had nothing prepared but had planned on leaving for thirteen days to L.A. with a client.

"I can't take him with me... this is not going to go well with his Dad so sick," I remember thinking.

I looked at him and I said, "I'm going to lock up all the equipment in a trailer and that'll at least be a start."

I did that, but I didn't know there was a second set of keys. Smarty-pants found the second set of keys, got rid of all the equipment and spent the entire fourteen days I was gone, getting high.

When I came home, all the equipment was gone. In fact, everything that he owned was gone.

I was standing there screaming, "Fuck!"

CrowFly had a show coming up in two weeks, and thousands and thousands of dollars of equipment is gone.

His Dad is really sick by then, and we go up to visit and his Dad is just, I mean, it's bad.

I'm saying to myself, "I don't know what I'm going to do because he's been using heroin, he's not going to stop, his Dad is going to die."

I said to Tim, "You need to be sober for your Dad, you need to be here."

I tried that, but it didn't work.

After his Dad passed, we had the funeral. But they had two funerals, one here in Florida and then one in Kentucky. We had just bought a pickup truck, it was brand new, and we drove to Kentucky.

We were supposed to fly but then he wanted to drive, Tim's son was coming from Colorado, and it was turning into a clusterfuck of who was doing what.

We drove to Kentucky, and after we get there, Tim seems perfectly normal.

I'm thinking, "Okay, this is good."

We did the family thing, stayed in the hotel, everything seemed fine, we go to leave and we're driving back to Florida after we took his son to the airport.

About two hours into the drive home, in a pouring down rainstorm on the highway on 95, still a couple hours from our house, he starts throwing up in the car.

"Great!" I'm thinking.

Once again, I thought he'd got it, he didn't get it.

I complained to him and told him straight up, "Your mom's going to bury you too!"

"Don't do this, you got to stop this, your mom's going to bury you, she just buried her husband, you don't want to do this to your mother."

Finally, he just looked at me and says quietly, "I can't quit, I don't know what to do."

"Okay," I say, "We're going to start to work together as a team and we're going to figure this out."

"Everywhere I go, you go, which means if I go to L.A., you go to L.A. If I need to go to Guam, you go to Guam."

And after that, he went with me everywhere I went for the next three months.

And finally, he started to become himself again.

Tim

After my Dad passed and Cali became ultra-determined to get me sober once and for all, my moods were awful. I mean, I am angry and pissed off at everybody.

And I'm never mad, I'm not a mad guy. I'm usually the funny one, you know, the comical one.

Cali was true to her word and dragged me everywhere she went, and I hated it. She would put me on the plane and I'd be detoxing on the plane.

I would lie at the airport under the seats and cover up my head because I was cold and sick. It went on like that for months and months.

I used to tell her all the time, "I'm not your little monkey."

She was adamant the whole time, "I'm not leaving you home alone to sit around and get high for three weeks while I'm gone."

I would get so mad at her because it's like heroin shuts the pleasure center of your brain down, hijacks it, and then you can only control your moods and all your pleasures with the drug itself.

When you're coming off it, that's one of the last things to correct itself. So, you don't have a whole lot of emotion, you could just be completely flatlined emotionally and it's so frustrating.

Things that used to make you laugh, don't make you laugh anymore; things that used to excite you, don't excite you anymore; and it's basically the last thing of your body to correct itself and come back on.

And when it does it's almost instant, you can feel it, it's just like a light switch that comes on.

I had no ambition to do anything. I was completely flatlined emotionally and it was a horrible, horrible, horrible feeling.

That's one of the things that recently keeps me clean, keeps me on the right path. I don't want to go through that entire period where you're just emotionally dead and stagnant.

Cali

Little bit by little bit Tim's personality came back and I kept reminding him, "You know, every time you use, musically you screw yourself up. You've got all these opportunities..."

CrowFly went out and they played with Stephen Pearcy from RATT, they met Peter DiStefano of Jane's Addiction and Nikki Sixx from Mötley Crüe.

"You have to be sober when you meet Nikki Sixx. If you are high off your rocker, he's going to know you're using heroin," I told him.

I think that's when I saw the change, the shift in his own determination to beat the drug.

I know he's not using opiates anymore. If he was using opiates, he wouldn't even know somebody was calling. He would be unfocused and gone, it's bizarre.

But, it's interesting, because when he's tired, I'm asking right away, "You're not using opiates, are you?"

He'll shoot back, "Oh, my god, Cali, come on!"

He wants to take a nap and it's six o'clock at night, "I'm almost fifty, if I want to take a fucking nap at six o'clock, let me take a fucking nap."

I'm always going to look for the signs he's using, yes, because we've been together for over ten years, four of those were heroin.

I'm always going to look for the missing money.

I'm going to be asking, "Where are you? You didn't answer the phone."

There's always going be that, because, in the back of my mind, there's no guarantee. He could really be playing music somewhere and I'm on a business trip and somebody offers him an Oxy and says, "Hey, here's an aspirin."

And he accidentally takes and Oxy. Or he says, you know, "It's just one, it won't hurt."

The cycle just starts all over again. He's right back into opiates and then we're fucked.

So, I'm always on the lookout for stuff, I'm always looking for signs. And it sucks, but that's kind of where we are.

Tim

I went to an addiction therapist for quite a while. And Cali set me up with an Addiction's Coach, someone other than her.

I'm anti-12-Step and I know I shouldn't say it like that because 12-Steps programs have saved a lot of lives. But it's just not for me. I'm jaded by some of the arrogance that I feel comes from that program.

I went through a 12-Step residential program, I got sentenced to one, six months – it was either that or go to prison.

I had this counselor tell me, straight to my face, "For the rest of your life you will never be allowed to have a sip of alcohol."

And I said, "You're fucking kidding me?!"

I was twenty-eight years old at the time I couldn't deal with knowing that for the rest of my fucking life I couldn't watch my favorite football team, the Dallas

Cowboys, on Sunday afternoon and have a beer or a glass of wine with my wife or my friends or whatever.

"Are you fucking out of your fucking mind?"

That was my train of thought.

I didn't know it back then, I thought 12-Step was the only option if someone needed to deal with their addiction or alcoholism. And now that I'm with my wife who's a Sober and Addiction's Coach, I've been turned on to harm reduction and different ways for people to stop the madness.

There are other ways for people to stop the self-destruction and for people to stop hurting their loved ones.

What works for you might not work for me and what works for me might not work for the next person and, 12-Steps feels to me like "it's my way or the highway" and I just don't like that, I just don't like it.

When I finally made the decision to get clean and get sober and get into recovery for real, not just faking it, I knew that one of these times my band's not going to be there or my buddy in Liberty City, Leggz, is not going to be there or my wife to save me.

I've been lucky that there have been people around me, but at the rate I was going, there will be a time, where I'm not going to have one of my loved ones around me and there's not going to be a damn thing that anybody's going to be able to do about it.

When I start keeping myself in that train of thought, that's when it starts getting a little scary and I start taking it a little more serious than I have been.

A big thing for me going forward clean and heroin-free is music. It really keeps me grounded, my band is phenomenal, and my bandmates are like brothers.

Playing music really takes me to a beautiful zone, always has. And the guys in the band are kind of my accountability partners.

None of them has ever done heroin, and they are super supportive of my efforts to stay clean. For a long time, they had no idea what to do, or what to say. They were a little afraid to call me out on my shit and didn't want to rat me out to Cali.

But, we're in a way better place now. Music is so powerful.

And then there's Cali. Her strengths are my exact weaknesses and my strengths are her weaknesses. It couldn't be a more perfect fit.

I've been in relationships, like my son's mother, and we both have the same strengths and weaknesses and it was a fucking train wreck.

I'm horrible with finances, money, and paying bills. And Cali is terrible with anything domesticated. I'm one of the most domesticated guys on the planet. She's brilliant when it comes to the financial or structural part of a marriage.

Here's a perfect example:

When I went to pick up our RV, there was an engine problem, but it was under warranty, so I knew it'd be fixed before I got to it. But I'm the type of guy who doesn't even know anything about the RV policy when it comes to the warranty. My job was to drive there and pick it up.

Cali is a car girl. She called them and said a bunch of stuff about it being a V10 and the seventh cylinder being stuck open and wondered if it was going to blow a rod.

I had no idea what she was talking about.

She can put makeup on and a mini-skirt on but doesn't have the baking and the cooking and the decorating side to her at all.

She doesn't even like jewelry. I've tried to buy her engagement rings, diamonds, everything, and she doesn't want them.

She says, "I'll just lose it."

The funny thing is, when we're not together, the other becomes completely unraveled. When I go on tour or when I was using heroin or detoxing, her surroundings would be in disarray.

I went on a short six-week tour and when I came back, the two dogs were looking at me, as if to say, "Don't ever leave us with this woman again."

Take out cartons were everywhere, laundry piled up high. I just wanted to come home from tour and relax and get back into a normal life. And it took me a week just to get the house in order.

There's no resentment, which I guess there might be with other couples.

We laugh at each other a lot. I jokingly gave her a hard time about her messes once and she said, "How much is the rent? How much is the car payment?"

I didn't know. Then I gladly and happily cleaned up her mess.

Cali

From the time of Tim's last overdose until today, I'm always stimulating him.

Instead of using drugs and alcohol, we do a ton of different things.

We travel to places like Hawaii, Colorado, and Las Vegas.

We get tattoos. Well, Tim does. He got his whole back inked one summer.

Tattoo work is expensive, and he would always say, "Well, I could be spending this on dope."

He is right, he could, so why not spend it on something more productive and less destructive.

We go to the gym all the time, challenging each other, sweating, getting naturally high on endorphins.

We'll fly to Dallas Cowboy games during football season and sometimes Tim will splurge and get front row tickets. He loves it and I love it too. It all keeps him looking forward to something, plugged in, and engaged. Without constant stimulation, we are in trouble.

He and his current band, CrowFly, are always recording, rehearsing, and touring all over. We bought a giant R.V. tour bus too, and we're always taking it somewhere, touring with the band.

We're always doing something and constantly changing it up. It can never be 9-5 for Tim, or me.

Tim's dopamine will fire off if he's just thinking about doing something exciting. He doesn't even have to be doing the activity. When I tell him we're going to Vegas, he's happy, he's excited, and his dopamine is firing.

It's good to have the Tim back that I knew and fell in love with back in New York. Tim the joker, Tim the goofball, Tim who will go ahead and get his nipples pierced to show his love for me.

EPILOGUE: Cali

Like every addict in recovery, Tim continues to have his up and down days, his struggles with triggers and cravings.

I think we are both fortunate that I am so connected to the world of addictions coaching and have lived through a prime example of what I help others with daily.

Tim now uses his experiences of drug use and abuse, along with his intimate knowledge of prison and the penal system, to connect on a level with my clients that I never could come close to achieving.

This connection gets them to listen to him, to understand there is a path, a way past their suffering. It's amazingly powerful to have him work with me at times. The clients just "get" him and he "gets" them in a way that is hard to explain.

When they meet someone, who has lived in their shoes, had similar experiences and stories, they are blown away. And in many cases, Tim outguns them with his crazy history of 24 felonies, 14 misdemeanors and flatlining multiple times, which leaves them hanging on every word he says.

For a long time, I was apprehensive about sharing my own personal story, but hopefully, this will inspire others to continue to be there, to help their loved ones find a path away from certain death.

I took these lessons and started learning and relearning everything I knew about addiction.

I started focusing on a whole-body approach. Not just a talk therapy and exercise concept but more.

I learned that between social/psychological history and chemistry there is a connection. What happens when you're growing up, if you're sick or not plays a role in how your body produces and processes things.

Trauma can be stored in the muscle tissue and if not released properly a drug like heroin will simply relax your muscles, so you don't feel the tense stress and trauma.

I started looking at all that and thought, Wow!

There is more to this than the addiction industry even offers or acknowledges.

From there I started using marijuana as a detox and then I would use vitamins and supplements to bring the body and brain back.

But it takes so long for that stuff to get in your system. It's not like you take a vitamin and you're bouncing back. It takes 30 days, or more, just to begin the process.

Addicts don't want to wait 30 minutes.

There are two types of addicts: downer addicts and upper addicts.

The uppers focused addict has a shortage of dopamine in their brain. They need to be stimulated constantly and more than the average person.

I stumbled onto Ken Blum's research on the dopamine shortage in the brain. I started reading his principles and it made sense. "The reward pleasure center," he said, "is smaller and must be stimulated more often."

These are the guys that jump out of planes, the guys that drive 100 mph.

That's also my husband. He has reward deficiency syndrome issues.

That describes my clients. They can't have just one bump of cocaine, they end up doing an 8-Ball. Or in the case of one of my guys, 14 grams. At one time.

The downer guys usually have a hidden trauma or past they are trying to escape from. This is the concept of much of Dr. Gabor Mate's work. He links trauma in the individual to addiction and he believes every addict has trauma.

Well, I am not sure of that, Tim didn't have any trauma. He had a great and amazing childhood. No drama, no trauma. Yet, he is still an addict. But his first love of drugs was for uppers which is in alignment with Dr. Blum's theory. When I work with clients, before I can help them find the right path to recovery, I try to figure out if it's either trauma or a dopamine shortage.

The more I learned about body chemistry, the more I learned how metabolic rates play a big role in drug addiction.

I started studying physical history, not just emotional. As professionals we ask what happened as a kid, was there trauma? We don't ask if you ate healthily or spent excessive amounts of time at the dentist or the doctor.

I feel that body chemistry is the missing link.

I immediately added this to my client protocols. What I learned over the past few years would be groundbreaking, allowing me to customize coaching programs depending not just on psychological issues, but physical as well.

Supplements and vitamins are paramount when it comes to reversing the damage done by using drugs, alcohol, and other toxic environmental influences.

I feel so strongly about this that I have teamed up with Karyn Hurley, Bachelor of Health Sciences, Certified Nutritional Coach, Master's NLP and Certified Holistic Professional, who has countless hours researching and then developing a line of nutritional supplements, Neuroevolution.

These products, which I have spent years vetting and utilizing on myself and my clients, are available on my Addictions Recovery and Sobriety Coaching website –

www.theaddictionscoach.com. They are specifically formulated to help support the damage from drugs and alcohol on the body and help people get their bodies back on track.

Along with proper nutrition, healing the gut, and regular exercise, I have been able to see dramatic and positive results. It is truly encouraging, especially with the addiction issues our nation currently faces.

By healing the body, we can heal the mind, they are intertwined. And for so long the addictions industry has been treating the head as separate from the body.

It's time to change this thinking.

THANK YOU!

Dr. Cali Estes and Tim Estes continue to celebrate Tim's recovery from heroin addiction at their home in Miami, Florida.

Tim plays drums professionally for a rock band, touring occasionally while pursuing his lifelong dream to be a musician.

Dr. Estes has focused her work on growing her Addictions Recovery Coaching business and The Addictions Academy in her quest to help as many individuals and families as she can find a path to freedom from their addiction challenges and pain.

You can learn more about Dr. Estes and her work at:

www.TheAddictionsCoach.com (for clients)
www.CaliEstes.com (for clients)
www.RehabRescue.Solutions (for Treatment Centers)
www.TheAddictionsAcademy.com (for students)
www.UnpauseYourLife.com (her podcast)

Thank you again for your support and you can get access to color photographs and more that were not included in the book at:

www.IMarriedAJunkie.com

Made in the USA
Columbia, SC
04 November 2019